JEST, SATIRE, IRONY
AND DEEPER SIGNIFICANCE

JEST, SATIRE, IRONY
AND
DEEPER SIGNIFICANCE

A Comedy in Three Acts

CHRISTIAN DIETRICH GRABBE

Translated, with an introduction, by
MAURICE EDWARDS

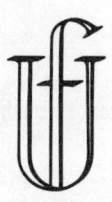

FREDERICK UNGAR PUBLISHING CO.
NEW YORK

All performance rights reserved

Anyone interested in
performance or public reading rights to this play
should contact
Frederick Ungar Publishing Co.
131 East 23rd Street, New York, N. Y. 10010
for permission.

Copyright © 1966 by
Frederick Ungar Publishing Co., Inc.

Printed in the United States of America

Library of Congress Catalog Card No. 66-19473

PREFACE

Fifteen years ago, the Interplayers, a pioneer off-Broadway group, was looking for a play similar to e. e. cummings' *Him*, their big success of the previous season. Much to everyone's surprise and bewilderment, Charles Laughton recommended *Jest, Satire, Irony and Deeper Significance* by Christian Dietrich Grabbe, a somewhat obscure German dramatist of the early nineteenth century. Laughton claimed that Grabbe's play was the closest dramatic work to *Him* with which he was familiar; and, as the only member of the company who knew German, I was asked to look up the play and report on it.

What a delight, then, to find this rough gem of a comedy—or, to be more explicit, this *satyr-play*—so modern in feeling, so brilliant a forerunner of the avant-garde theater of our time! Mr. Laughton was right: *Jest* was unique. And though no German scholar, I plunged into translating it.

Unfortunately, by the time the first draft was finished, the Interplayers had suffered drastic reverses and did not dare launch such an oddity. If Eric Bentley had not shown up then to direct a play by a somewhat better-known German writer, Bertolt Brecht, *Jest* might have been lost to English readers for even longer. But, after reading the translation, Bentley asked to include it in the second volume of his series, *From the Modern Repertoire*.

Now, in this individual edition of *Jest*, made available by Frederick Ungar, I have reworked and considerably improved my original translation. In addition, I have incorporated into the text those more ribald passages censored by Grabbe's first publisher, Kettembeil, and which did not appear even in German until 1960, in Alfred Bergmann's transcription of the original handwritten manuscript.* Still better, here is an occasion to introduce the American reader to a truly unique writer.

New York, 1966 MAURICE EDWARDS

---

* Grabbe, Christian D.: *Werke und Briefe.* Historisch-Kritische Gesamtausgabe in sechs Bänden, hrsg. von der Akademie der Wissenschaften in Göttingen. Bearbeitet von Alfred Bergmann. Emsdetten, Lechte, 1960-63.

INTRODUCTION

CHRISTIAN DIETRICH GRABBE (1801–1836) is one of that triumvirate of remarkable German dramatists of the early nineteenth century—Heinrich von Kleist and Georg Büchner being the other two—who were neglected in their day and did not begin to come into their own until the twentieth century. They belong to what George Steiner has aptly called "that family of hectic genius which German literature brought forth after Goethe and Schiller, like conflagrations after a great noon." It has taken another fifty years or so for them to become known in England and America, although the French have been aware of their genius for some time.* With Kleist's *The Broken Jug* having been performed at the Phoenix Theatre in New York, and Büchner's *Danton's Death* opening the 1965-66 season at Lincoln Center, it is to be hoped that Grabbe, too, will soon win a similar hearing.

Part of the problem, of course, has been translation. Until this writer's first version of *Jest, Satire, Irony and Deeper Significance*, nothing of Grabbe's had appeared in English except for a few fragments from his minor play *Aschenbrödel (Cinderella)*, translated by Longfellow.† Nor was his name to be found anywhere except in encyclopedias and histories of German literature or, if one dug back far enough, in the files of English periodicals of the 1840's and 1850's.

---

* Alfred Jarry (1873–1907), father of the French avant-garde drama, translated parts of Grabbe's *Jest* in 1900 under the title *Les Silènes*; several acts of his *Napoleon* had been translated even earlier, and, of course, both Büchner and Kleist are part of the repertoire of the Théâtre National Populaire.
† Longfellow, Henry W.: *Poets and Poetry of Europe*, 1845.

Even in Germany, Grabbe's reputation has been subject to vicissitudes in taste and the ever-fickle *Zeitgeist*. For example, Grabbe's first two plays, *Herzog Theodor von Gothland* (*Duke Theodore of Gothland*) and *Jest*, created quite a stir in manuscript form among the literary circles of Leipzig and Berlin; and when in 1827 they were published, a number of critics hailed the young writer. The Frankfurt journal *Iris* even called him "the Messiah of the German stage." Yet only one play by Grabbe—*Don Juan und Faust*—was produced during his lifetime.

Indeed, outside of a few biographies, Grabbe the playwright was practically forgotten until the latter years of the century when, with the rise of naturalism, the first collected editions of his works and letters, along with tentative critical studies of the author, began to appear. The Grabbe cause received still more impetus with the resounding success of *Jest* at its première in Munich, on May 27, 1907, eighty-five years after it had been written.[*]

Then, with the advent of expressionism and the outbreak of World War I, Grabbe began to be idolized by the avant-garde. But even here it was perhaps his unhappy "artist's life" more than his work that aroused interest. One of the first expressionist plays, *Der Einsame* (*The Lonely One*) by Hans Johst (1917), was based on Grabbe's life—which Johst saw as a paradigm of the creative writer unappreciated by the public of his time, and who wasted away his genius in drink. (It was supposedly in reaction to the sentimental excesses of this play that Bertolt Brecht wrote his *Baal* (1920). In *Baal*, however, the tormented artist is closer to Rimbaud than Grabbe in character.)

There was another upswing of interest in Grabbe during the

---

[*] According to Alfred Bergmann, the actual première was a private performance in the Salon of the Akademie-Theater in Vienna, on December 7, 1876.

1920's, when his historical plays *Hannibal* * and *Napoleon, or the Hundred Days* were performed; but it was not until after World War II that a real Grabbe renaissance took place, with *Don Juan und Faust* and even *Die Hermannsschlacht* (*The Battle of Arminius*)—the latter had previously been dismissed as a failure—joining the historical plays and *Jest* as part of the current German repertoire.

It is apparent that even today Grabbe is still regarded as essentially an "anti-Establishment" writer. For, in spite of these surges of interest in Germany—evidenced by new editions of his work, renewed appreciations, revivals, and suchlike—academic circles continue to shy away from his so-called excesses of style and content, while the standard histories of German literature, especially those published in the United States, allot him only a paragraph or so and still tend to dismiss him as something of a "literary abortion"—a phrase first coined by *The Athenaeum* in 1856.

Of course critics more attuned to the times, as well as venturesome theatrical spirits, recognize Grabbe as an important member of what Eric Bentley has dubbed the "underground tradition" of German drama—that extraordinary group of playwrights, starting with Lenz and Klinger, who are generally thought of as minor satellites of the *Sturm und Drang* period: Heinrich von Kleist, neglected during the classic Goethe-Schiller heyday; Grabbe and Büchner, overlooked during the spate of late romanticism and the beginnings of the new realism; Wedekind, the scandal-maker at the turn of the century, admittedly nourished by his neglected predecessors; and finally, those of modern times, Kraus, Sternheim, Kaiser, and Brecht. This "dark lineage" of German anti-Establishment writers who paved the

---

* Helge Hultberg claims that Brecht attempted a new version of *Hannibal* for Reinhardt, but only finished a small part of it (*Die Aesthetischen Anschauungen Bertolt Brechts*).

way for much of modern drama and even some of the "Theater of the Absurd," deserves a study in itself.*

It is to be hoped that, with this revised translation of *Jest*, Grabbe may begin to receive the belated recognition he deserves.† The brief biography and notes on *Jest, Satire, Irony and Deeper Significance* which follow are intended as a first step in that direction.

GRABBE was born on December 11, 1801, in Detmold, capital of the small state of Lippe-Detmold (Westphalia), then ruled over by the liberal, reform-conscious Princess Pauline. His father was the local prison warden; his mother, an austere, simple peasant woman from a nearby village. The late and only child of their marriage, Grabbe, echoing Goethe, claimed to have inherited industry and intellect from his father, and the temperament and sensitivity of his mother. One thing he did not inherit was his mother's peasant strength: she outlived both husband and son.

Grabbe's family background, and the prison atmosphere of his home (it was attached to the prison enclosure), do not seem to have had any traumatic effect on him, though in later years, when down-and-out, he is said to have lamented, "What should

---

* Considerable groundwork for such a study has been laid in Georg Lukács' *Sociology of Modern Drama* (1909). Here Lukács rates Grabbe as one of the pioneers of what he termed the "new drama," i.e., bourgeois, historicist, the drama of individualism: "In the new drama not merely passions are in conflict but ideologies, *Weltanschauungen*, as well."

† My first version of *Jest* appeared in Eric Bentley's *From the Modern Repertoire* (Series II, 1952). In 1955, England's Gaberbocchus Press published Barbara Wright's *abridged* version under the title *Comedy, Satire, Irony and Deeper Meaning*. (In Miss Wright's version no *scenes* are omitted, but many passages are cut or condensed, especially those satirizing the literature of their period—necessary steps, perhaps, for a *stage* version of the play.) In 1963, my translation of *Don Juan and Faust* appeared in Oscar Mandel's anthology, *The Theatre of Don Juan* (University of Nebraska Press)—M. E.

become of a man whose first memory is that of an old murderer being led for a walk in the open air?" Yet, from what we know of Grabbe's childhood, it is unlikely that his doting parents allowed him any traffic with the prison inmates. In fact he led a rather sheltered life, partly due to a weak physical constitution, partly because he was an only child.

Anxious to rise above their professional if not social status, Grabbe's parents worked very hard. His father advanced from warden to superintendent of the prison, later serving as an official in a loan bank, undertook collections, and handled auctions. In due time, their "beloved Christian" was sent to the local *Gymnasium*, where he got along very well in his studies, though less well with his peers. Withdrawn and lonely, he would watch his fellow students' interplay from the sidelines. Even as a youngster, Grabbe developed a reputation for eccentric, often crude behavior—the disapproving townsfolk called him "that crazy Christian." And, it was before leaving school, that he began to drink.

Fortunately, however, the local archivist, Christian Gottlieb Clostermeier—Grabbe's future father-in-law, and a minor historian in his own right—took an early interest in the boy's education and development. Through Princess Pauline, he obtained a grant for him, and off Grabbe went to the University of Leipzig.

Though no longer the "Little Paris" of Goethe's youth, Leipzig was still an exciting metropolis to the young Grabbe. There, in spite of his solitary, taciturn, somewhat inhibited manner, he soon found himself in a circle of congenial students who encouraged his writing. He had already finished two plays before leaving Detmold, one of which—the lost *Theodora*, composed at sixteen—was turned down by Leipzig publishers. He had also started sketches for *Gothland*. Now, at the expense of his law studies, he finished that enormous, sprawling drama. Before long he was able to report to his parents: "My work gradually creates for me more and more friends, acquaintances, and admirers. . . . A Dr. Gustav told me that my things, once one of them was published, would bring high prices." *

But reality proved more prosaic. While Grabbe got to know many people, some influential, he found no patron earnest enough to help him concretely. Finally, after an abortive effort to be hired as an actor, he transferred in the spring to Berlin for further studies and more productive contacts.

Even in the Prussian capital, already more of a literary center than Leipzig, Grabbe's reputation as the author of *Gothland* had preceded him, and it gained him quick entrée into the literary salons. Here he met, among others, the poet Heine, and it was in Berlin too, stimulated by his environment, that Grabbe wrote *Jest, Satire, Irony and Deeper Significance*. Dashed off in an amazingly short time, it skillfully satirized, among other things, the very circles he was moving in.

But much as *Gothland* and *Jest* (to a lesser extent) impressed some readers, they also frightened away others—especially prospective publishers. Heine reports in his *Memoirs* how, after he had passed *Gothland* on to her for perusal, Rahel von Varnhagen summoned him at midnight and begged him, "for God's sake take away that dreadful manuscript," as she could not sleep as long as it remained in her house.

Meanwhile, how was he to live? After the stipend ran out, and his parents had sent him their last savings, Grabbe's father reminded him: "We can do no more as parents. Your mother and I believe that as your student year is up this Easter, you should take your examinations here [that is, in Detmold]; we do not doubt for a moment that you will do well in them."

Suddenly the Bohemian tinsel of his life fell away. No longer, he realized, could he live on false hopes and dreams. He decided to try his hand again at acting, and turned to Ludwig Tieck. Next to the aging Goethe, Tieck was then the leading scion of

---

* This letter, and subsequent quotations from letters, are based on those appearing in volumes V and VI of the Wukadinovic edition of Grabbe's collected works (Deutsches Verlaghaus, Bong & Co., 1912).

German letters, especially in matters of the drama. He had read the manuscript of *Gothland* * and, recognizing some extraordinary quality in the young writer, invited him to Dresden. Unfortunately, Tieck did not turn out to be the sympathetic elder counselor Grabbe had hoped to find. Well past his own Bohemian period, Tieck probably expected more of a sycophant than the proud, iconoclastic Grabbe turned out to be. Besides, Tieck presided over a fashionable salon to which the young writer, who was more at ease drinking in the nearby tavern, clearly did not belong. As Grabbe wrote later: "I'd rather be a lawyer in Detmold than a poet in Dresden."

Tieck soon realized it was quite out of the question to bring Grabbe, with his "loathsome diction," into the Dresden *Hoftheater*, but he did give him excellent introductions to several other theaters in Germany. None of these, however, came to anything. Grabbe's contemporaries seemed to agree that he had some talent for burlesque, perhaps, but no real gift for acting; and, after fruitless sallies into Leipzig, Braunschweig, and Hanover, Grabbe had no choice but to return home, in August, 1823.

> So I sneaked back into cursed Detmold about eleven o'clock at night, woke my parents out of their sleep, and they, whose entire small fortune I had drained away, whom I had disappointed so often with empty hopes, who because of me were scorned by half the town, received me with tears of joy.

This period was certainly the loneliest and most painful Grabbe had yet experienced. Hurt by his failure to make a place for himself either in the literary world or on the stage, the magnificent spurt of creativity that had brought forth the five thousand verses of *Gothland*, the brilliant satire of *Jest*, a minor effort called *Nannette und Maria*, and the promising fragment, *Marius und Sulla*, suddenly dried up.

Now, Grabbe continued merely to exist. Torn, hard pressed,

---

* Grabbe was later to use Tieck's on the whole favorable critique of *Gothland* as an introduction to the first edition of his works.

moody, distrusting his every turn of thought, he doubted the impulse of his very soul and took refuge in orgies of drink. He thought he would never adjust to Detmold's provincialism. Then suddenly, in 1824, he astonished the local burghers by returning to his law studies, passing the very difficult local law examinations, and gaining the status of solicitor in his home town.

Once he had opened his own law office, Grabbe was completely rehabilitated in the eyes of his fellow citizens. In no time at all he had plenty of business. Soon he was also given the work of the local military auditor, with jurisdiction over twelve hundred soldiers, and eventually, when the sick old auditor died, he took over his official title as well. But while this work eased his financial problems, made him self-sufficient, and brought him bourgeois recognition, it did not alleviate his depression:

> My condition is tolerable, and I also make a tolerable living—but I am not happy and suppose I never shall be again. I believe, hope, wish for, love, respect, hate *nothing*, but rather only despise as ever the *commonplace*; I am as indifferent to myself as if I were a third party; I have read thousands of books, but none engages me; fame and honor even are stars to which I wouldn't aspire; I'm convinced I can do everything I want, but it doesn't seem worth the effort, and I don't even try.

What finally broke the spell was a letter from his Leipzig friend, Kettembeil, now in Frankfurt-am-Main, who proposed publishing Grabbe's plays in two volumes. "Dear Kettembeil," Grabbe replied, "Yours has been a voice in the wilderness to me. . . . My year-long practice of pouring reason like nitric acid on my feelings seems to be nearing its end: reason is poured out and feeling is destroyed. . . . To impart this to you, friend, is for me a kind of relief."

Grabbe immediately started assembling his old manuscripts for publication and returned to his writing. Within six weeks, he finished that remarkable baroque fantasia, *Don Juan und Faust*. About the same time, he wrote his hortatory essay "Ueber die Shakspearo-Manie" ("On the Shakespeare Mania") for inclusion in the two volumes Kettembeil was to issue in the late fall of 1827 under the title *Dramatische Dichtungen (Dramatic Works)*.

The plays were received with enthusiasm. Grabbe became well known overnight. And with the publication of *Don Juan und Faust* the following year, his future seemed assured. Things looked even brighter when the local Detmold *Hoftheater*, built only about two years earlier, put on *Don Juan und Faust*, with incidental music by Lortzing.*

All this had its effect: Grabbe drank less, dressed better, and worked enthusiastically at both his job and his plays. Between 1827 and 1831 he wrote three major historical dramas: *Kaiser Friedrich Barbarossa*, its sequel, *Kaiser Heinrich VI* (parts of a planned Hohenstaufen cycle of eight plays), and *Napoleon, or the Hundred Days*. He also composed the first draft of a "dramatic fairy tale," *Cinderella*, and the fragment, *Kosciuszko*.

But this period of relative peace and confidence did not last. After *Don Juan und Faust*, his reputation as a writer began to wane. *Barbarossa* caused hardly a ripple; *Heinrich VI*, even less. Grabbe complained to Kettembeil: "Literature has become a sea in which one can no longer discern the gulf streams. There is also some envy of me in the air." To his friend Menzel, he confided: "I've had a difficult year. . . . The gout is gone, but nerve attacks still hit me every four weeks with terrifying force. At the same time, as local auditor here, more military business than ever. . . . You'd like to see me more popular. Rightly so.— But more theatrical? More in the mode of the current theater?

---

* Though withdrawn for obscure reasons after the first night, and forbidden further performances, *Don Juan und Faust* made a brilliant impression on the town, and even showed promise of a good box office. It was played later that same year in Lüneburg, and three years later in Augsburg—the only play by Grabbe that was performed during his lifetime.

—I believe our theater must better accommodate the poets." Grabbe would not compromise his artistic integrity. "The theater of today is good for nothing—mine is the world," he announced. His was indeed the theater of the future. But that did not help him in his world, in his time.

Napoleon, or the Hundred Days, the play he was working on then, was to move farther from the theater of his time than anything he had written thus far. While *Gothland* was shocking in content and expression, it still retained the outward form of the Fate tragedy that it superseded. Similarly *Jest*, for all its originality, had features in common with the literary satire of the period. *Don Juan und Faust*, its strongly nihilistic tone and grandiose pessimism notwithstanding, was written in Schilleresque blank verse, and its plot structure and scenic components were fairly conventional.

But with *Barbarossa* and *Heinrich VI*,* Grabbe began to break new ground, while, with *Napoleon*, he finally found his stride and achieved his own style. For *Napoleon* he abandoned blank verse; as he wrote to Kettembeil, he "could not very well have artillery trains talk in iambics." The result is the terse, racy dialogue—the so-called lapidary prose—for which Grabbe is now justly famous.

Concomitantly with this change in diction came a change in form. *Napoleon* has no plot to speak of, but is rather what Lukács would call a "drama of milieu," and what is now generally classified as "epic theater." † Nor is Napoleon himself a conventional hero; he does not carry the action—history does.

---

* Ironically enough, during the Bismarckian period, Grabbe's two Hohenstaufen plays were considered his most solid achievement, probably because they could be fitted into the patriotic mold.
† This no doubt harked back to the cinema-like style of Goethe's *Götz von Berlichingen* and Shakespeare's historical plays, but Grabbe arrived at it in his own way, and his technique is actually quite different. As Lukács points out: "This much-heightened sense of the significance of milieu enables it to function as a dramatic element."

Yet Grabbe does not try to present historical events in a causal chain: they just happen. At the same time, the scenes are linked together by numerous cross references, lending the play a sense of unity that is quite unclassical. Thus *Napoleon* paved the way for Büchner's *Danton's Death* (1835) and Grabbe's own *Hannibal* (1836)—and, through these, for the "drama of the future."

Yet, if at this period of his creativity Grabbe was approaching his height as a writer, his life was falling apart all around him. His *Napoleon* did not conquer the world; nor had Grabbe any desire to go on with the rest of the Hohenstaufen cycle, in spite of Kettembeil's urging. His health was worse than ever, and his work as auditor began to suffer. Thinking that perhaps he ought to marry and settle down, he ended up courting two women almost at the same time. Shortly after asking Luise Clostermeier (daughter of his one-time patron) for her hand and being turned down, he fell in love (or thought he did) with a simple country girl, Henriette Meyer.

What went wrong with the abortive romance with Henriette we do not know, except that she broke the engagement twice and finally fled to Stolzenau to escape Grabbe's persistent importuning. So he went back to courting Luise, ten years his senior, whose mother had died in the interim. Six months later, after Grabbe's father had died—apparently the last barrier to Grabbe's respectability in Luise's patrician eyes—she dropped all objections and, in March, 1833, they married. "And so, now misfortune!" cried Grabbe, as they left the church.

After only a few months, they began to quarrel bitterly. Luise turned out to be not only a bluestocking but also a veritable shrew, who nagged him day and night, hated his mother, and begrudged him the dowry she had brought into the marriage and which was being eaten up faster than she had expected. Their Strindberglike relationship no doubt hastened Grabbe's physical breakdown and the collapse of his morale. He abandoned the almost-completed *Kosciuszko* and neglected his official work to an alarming degree. Before long he had to ask for an extended leave from his post as auditor, at the end of which he was quietly dismissed.

Less than three weeks later, unable to bear living in Detmold any longer with a nagging wife and without a job, he packed the manuscript of his new, half-finished tragedy, *Hannibal*, and fled to Frankfurt, where he looked up his publisher. But the changes Kettembeil wanted, Grabbe refused to make. They also quarreled over money; and then Grabbe fell ill once more.*

In real desperation now, he turned to his last hope, the writer Karl Immermann, director of the State Theater in Düsseldorf, for help. Immermann was shocked to learn of Grabbe's pitiable straits, and though he had only met him once some years before when passing through Detmold, he immediately answered his call by inviting him to Düsseldorf. Since that meeting, Immermann, together with Felix Mendelssohn-Bartholdy, had taken over artistic direction of the State Theater in Düsseldorf and accomplished miracles. It was one of the few theaters in Germany where commercial standards did not prevail, where the prompter was invisible and inaudible to the audience, and where actors really had to learn their parts. Immermann aimed at a repertoire that would feature the best of the past along with the best of the present.

The meeting of these two artists promised great things. Immermann himself was no mean writer; in addition to two first-rate novels, he had written several plays. He had also issued a prolegomena, "The Raging Ajax," for the new drama, that paralleled Grabbe's "On the Shakespeare-Mania." Both were protests against the blind Shakespeare cult of the time; both called for spontaneity of expression, and asked the German writer to find his sources in his own land.

---

* There is considerable disagreement in the literature on Grabbe as to just what disease he had. Some authorities contend that he caught syphilis in Leipzig or Berlin; others, that he died of drink. He may have had tuberculosis of the spine. In any case, at this point in his life, there is no doubt he was seriously ill.

Immermann was as solid in real life as in literature. True to his word, he did everything he could to set Grabbe up in Düsseldorf and give him a fresh start. He always had a seat for him at his theater. In fact, due to this theatergoing, Grabbe wrote his articles on "The Theater in Düsseldorf"—a series that contains some of the best dramatic criticism in German since Lessing's *Hamburg Dramaturgy*.

Under Immermann's encouragement and thoughtful criticism, Grabbe also began an intensive reworking of *Hannibal*. Immermann convinced him it should be in prose. Grabbe agreed: "Should one wear the old trousers forever?" and went to work with enthusiasm. "Hannibal will be the best thing I have written," he wrote to his friend Petri, in Detmold.

In some respects, it was his masterpiece. Here the style he had developed in *Napoleon* was used even more tellingly. Again, the history-making man stands at the center of the action; again the protagonist is defeated by historical realities and the circumstances against which he is pitted. But *Hannibal* is more sparse, every detail counts; the action is tight and compact.

Hannibal goes to his doom largely through the pettiness of his own people, who fail to recognize the moment of their own greatness—"the insignificant end in the immeasurable chaos of the Commonplace," as Grabbe described it in one of his letters.

However, *Hannibal* was not Grabbe's sole concern during those heady days in Düsseldorf. Immermann reports that all Grabbe needed was a word or hint to make him productive. He started a translation of *Hamlet* that Immermann was to stage. He began to rework *Cinderella*. A play on Alexander the Great started to take shape in his mind.

But this idyllic state could not last. First of all, Grabbe's health was too far gone. And again his tactlessness stood in his way. Some of Grabbe's reviews of the Düsseldorf Theater were too sharp in tone, too compromising for his friend who was, after all, director of the theater! Immermann particularly resented Grabbe's attack on his repertory system. For example,

Grabbe asked why the theater did not present Molière in adequate translations, and why it did not present the plays of Holberg and Gozzi instead of inferior works by Töpfer and Raupach. He might well have asked why Immermann did not produce *Hannibal* or *Don Juan und Faust*! Finally, Immermann had no choice but to write Grabbe a formal letter asking him not to publish any more criticism, or, if he did, to watch the tone of his future articles.

Their break was further hastened by Grabbe's drifting back into drink. With the publication of *Hannibal* and the reworked *Cinderella* (June, 1835), as well as his articles on the theater, Grabbe found numerous admirers at the local literary tavern, the "Drachenfels." Among these was the highly talented, twenty-six-year-old composer, Norbert Burgmüller, whose compositions are only now beginning to enjoy a revival. For him, Grabbe wrote a parody-opera libretto, *Der Cid*—a satyr-play, which does not quite come off, based on the Corneille tragedy.

Burgmüller's sudden death in May, 1836, was a great blow to Grabbe: it was like a rehearsal of his own. Again the poet was alone. Nothing bound him to Düsseldorf any more—not even his new publisher, Schreiner. And his health continued to decline.

A few weeks later, with some advances from Schreiner on his last play, *The Battle of Arminius*, Grabbe left Düsseldorf and returned, on May 26, 1836, to Detmold for the last time. "I'll not move back into my house and my chagrin until Arminius is finished," he had written Petri. And so he spent a sad, sick two months in the local inn. He had no more money. Schreiner refused to grant any more advances. Only Petri stood by to the end, helping mark down the final revisions when Grabbe could no longer lift his pen. On July 21, Grabbe's swan song was completed.

Under these circumstances, it is understandable that *Arminius* did not surpass *Napoleon* or *Hannibal*, as Grabbe confidently hoped it would. Its dramatic impact is dissipated by a plethora of scenes which seldom lend force to the central conflict. Yet

The Battle of Arminius remains an important part of Grabbe's *oeuvre*, even of German drama; for it is absolutely original and does not repeat any scenic conventions from Grabbe's previous work or from that of any other writer. It is rather a step into the future, a feeling-out of new territory. Gerhart Hauptmann remarked on reading this play in his old age (about 1944) that fifty years or so before him, "Grabbe already strove for that near-reality in characterization and dialogue that was called 'Naturalism' "—and which he himself had achieved.

But the time had come for Grabbe to leave the inn and return to his own home. He was ready to die. And yet, although he had warned his wife several days in advance of his plans, it was only with the help of a locksmith that he was finally able to reenter his home. Even then, Luise could not restrain herself from quarreling with him. The biographies leave us with the impression that her screaming must have served as an ugly accompaniment to his final suffering. That may be why he reputedly sang an aria from *Don Giovanni*, as well as the "Marseillaise," three days before he died.

Luise refused to allow Grabbe's mother to see her son until the final day, when at last she relented. The old woman entered the house, sat down on the bed, and wiped the sweat from her son's brow. He died in her arms on September 12, 1836.

NOTES ON *JEST*

"Wherein the comic is capped by the grotesque, irony tips the wit, and satire is a naked sword."
—George Meredith

Jest, Satire, Irony and Deeper Significance, Grabbe's only comedy, was probably written in the summer of 1822, during the first months of his sojourn in Berlin. On September 2, 1822, Grabbe wrote his parents: "In fourteen days I shall have finished a comedy from which most people expect even more than from my tragedy." From other correspondence we know that by November *Jest* was definitely finished. The author was just twenty-one.

Thus *Jest* followed right on the heels of Grabbe's tragedy, his powerful first play, *Gothland*.* The two plays were no doubt born of the same urge; one might say that *Jest* served as an esthetic purging of the bloodbath that was *Gothland*. As Grabbe maintained in one of his letters, "The comedy follows Gothland, arising, it is true, out of the very same basic insights, but, in its outer, absurdly comic aspect, [is] a total *contrast* to the so tragic Gothland. Contrasts affect dumb people first; children

---

* *Herzog Theodor von Gothland* (*Duke Theodore of Gothland*) was conceived when Grabbe was barely sixteen, largely written by the time he was eighteen, but not actually finished until he was twenty-one (June 11, 1822). It has not yet been translated. Though couched in the form of the conventional Fate drama of that time, it turned out to be quite unique—a penetrating exploration of the ego and a ruthless analysis of its destruction, with some striking affinities to Shakespeare's *Titus Andronicus*.

paint black next to white—now most people are dumb, thus pp.* When all else is lacking, *impress* we must."

In another letter, Grabbe insisted the comedy in *Jest* was "at root but the laughter of despair"—jest, satire, and irony being the outer forms of the problem with which he was still wrestling. But the two plays are related in other ways as well. *Gothland* is also a protest against the times and the then current literature. Only in *Jest* this protest is more obvious—indeed, sometimes very explicit.

Yet, on the surface, *Jest* is similar to many of the plays it exposes to ridicule. We see a young woman courted by three men—the first thirsting for her money, the second lusting for her body, only the third wanting her heart and soul! An intrigue with several subplots is set in motion, but is easily thwarted. The man with the inner values, though ugliest in looks, wins the hand of the young baroness; while the *intrigants* are put to shame, and go off empty-handed at the end.

How is this charming *soufflé* to be compared to the shattering *Gothland*, that "curious document of the lower regions of the soul," as Immermann has described it? In what way was Grabbe justified in claiming that *Jest* arose out of the same "basic insights," or in calling it a "laughter of despair"?

First of all, the title indicates that there is a "deeper significance" hidden somewhere between the jest and the irony, the satire and the farce.† It is in the tradition of German comedy to hide philosophic depth beneath comic robes. Perhaps behind the robes we may find those "basic insights"; but in doing so, we can be certain the author has set some intriguing traps and posed some amusing ambiguities.

We realize that some symbolic gesture is implied when

---

* Abbreviation of pianissimo. Grabbe here insinuates: "therefore, let us keep quiet about it," or simply "hush."
† The modern French translation of the title reads *"significance cachée,"* i.e., *hidden* meaning.

Grabbe in his own person comes on the stage immediately before the final curtain. With this twist at the denouement, the author seems to be saying that the play is not yet finished, that the real story has only just begun. Alfred Bergmann, one of the leading Grabbe authorities in Germany today, and editor of the definitive edition of his works, suggests that the author hints at this deeper significance in the long diversion (Act II, Scene 2) during which Ratbane, the poet, meets the Devil, and is given a Cook's tour of heaven, earth, and hell.

From this key position, meaning spreads to illuminate what has gone before and what is yet to come. Ratbane can be considered here as the representative of earthly knowledge of the world; the Devil, of universal knowledge. Ratbane assumes with absolute confidence that it is possible to know the essence of the world. "What a question!" he tells the Devil. "The world is the essence of all existence, from the smallest worm to the most immense solar system."

But from the Devil's superior vantage point, the poet's perception turns out to be shockingly limited and earthbound: "So let me tell you, then, that this essence of the All which you honor with the name 'world,' is nothing more than a mediocre, indifferent comedy . . . smeared together during vacations by a beardless, loud-mouthed angel who, if I'm not mistaken, is still in the twelfth grade and lives in the ordinary world that is incomprehensible to man."

With this answer, the Devil first crushes man's conceit over the presumed range, the alleged universality of human knowledge. Then, when he calls Ratbane's world a "mediocre, indifferent comedy," he shatters the poet's complacently optimistic view that his, Ratbane's, is the best of all possible worlds. For the Devil lets him know in no uncertain terms that even though man thinks he can grasp the totality of the All, he is actually purblind. After this "shattering" revelation, Ratbane breathlessly questions the Devil further—about heaven, hell, literature, and all that he once held sacred—only to find each pillar of faith an illusion, and man's boldly presumptuous and inflated concept of himself deflated to a laughable nothingness by the Devil.*

Of course, we know that Grabbe is poking fun at that earnest striving of the great Romantics to penetrate the meaning of the unknowable. And our writer feels perfectly justified in having his Virgil lead his Dante into these absurdities, paradoxes, and contradictions: where else can the Romantics end but in the hopeless task of trying to define and describe the "Unnameable"?

Thus, with a satanic twist, the Devil gives us a brilliant negation of the much-vaunted Romantic values by means of comic terms. We begin to see why Heine admired the "inner iciness" of Grabbe's Devil, as he called it. At one time or another, all our illusions are punctured and our conventional values thoroughly unmasked. The grandiose absurdity of Gothland's tragic world—its *allmächtiger Wahnsinn* or omnipotent madness—is turned upside down in *Jest* to become a veritable madhouse world of comedy.

The multiple meanings of the play—its hydra-headed significance †—now become more easily discernible. The sometimes almost painful irony of the otherwise conventional plot and fairy-tale kind of intrigue begins to make its diverse points. Are the couple really happily united at the end? In view of what the Devil has to offer, a little moment of happiness on earth may prove meaningless when set beside an eternity of *ennui* in hell. Or, if hell is what the Devil says it is, is that so bad? Does the take-off on science mean that no matter how much we search (or research), true knowledge will always elude us? What is the deeper meaning of the grotesque view of education propounded here? Is it that the little Gottliebs of this world can

---

* This colloquy mirrors in comically absurd fashion the terrifying dialogues on God, Time, and Existence between Gothland and Berdoa, the Moor, in *Herzog Theodor von Gothland*.
† In one of his letters, Grabbe claimed he had five souls in his head: *"fünf Seele im Kopfe"*!

never learn? And so on, *ad infinitum*, as we peel the elusive layers of hidden meaning!

We see why it was necessary to bring the Devil, a creature from another world, into the play—simply to lend credence to our "bifocal" view of the world. For, does not the Devil maintain that there is still another world which is eternally closed to human understanding?

But this Devil is no ordinary devil: he looks like a child, not a man; later we find out he has just run away from his grandmother, a beautiful young woman dressed in the height of Russian fashion. It is also no accident that the Devil introduces himself as a bishop: who but the Church could be expected to answer to life's mysteries?

We also see why it is misleading to categorize *Jest* as a "literary comedy": it is much more—a satire not only of literature, but of society, religion, even the world as a whole. Of course, at the same time, the literary-critical element plays no small role.

Grabbe came in at the very end of the great Romantic movement. The old masters—Novalis, Tieck, E. T. A. Hoffmann, Jean Paul Richter, Brentano, and others—were being supplanted by the so-called "pseudoromantics." These latecomers reduced the once important and meaningful symbols of yearning to facile external tricks and devices. Stylish modes determined the typical stage repertoire of Fate tragedies, sentimental comedies, and the quasi-historical dramas of the Epigones. In the novel, van der Velde filled the role of a German Walter Scott; criticism was epitomized by the easy slogan; while the bluestocking female writer dominated taste. It was a period of *kitsch*.

Grabbe proceeded with relish to unmask these fleeting phenomena of the literary world. Most of the poets and writers who had suffered his barbs—many of them members of the once fashionable Dresden *Liederkreis*—have long since been forgotten. At the same time, he was not afraid to poke fun at those two giants, Goethe and Schiller.

Grabbe was no doubt further stimulated by the puppet plays of his friend Köchy (whom he had met in Berlin), which apparently merged the expressive tricks of Italian improvisatory comedy and the *commedia dell'arte* with the eccentric style of the marionette theater.* Here Grabbe learned the effectiveness of parody and grotesque caricature, plus the age-old value of low comedy jokes, tricks, and horseplay as instruments of satirical theater. How else could Baron Murdrax murder thirteen apprentice tailors so expeditiously in the second scene of the third act?

Of course the tradition of the Grotesque can be traced even farther back to the old German carnival plays (*Fastnachtspiele*), the medieval mysteries and magical farces, as well as to the just as ancient popular folk puppet plays.† Such a gesture as that of the Devil ripping off his arm in the first act of *Jest* and beating the guests with it may well derive from an old *Faustbuch* (Faust book). Some of these elements had begun to creep politely into the romantic literary satires of the turn of the century, such as Tieck's *Der gestiefelte Kater* (*Puss-in-Boots*, 1797), where we find a breakdown of the frontiers between audience and actors, with the author speaking to the audience from the stage, as well as to his actors and the stagehands. In Tieck's *Die verkehrte Welt* (*Topsy-Turvy World*, 1799), the spectators actually storm the stage and take sides in a fight. And so by Grabbe's time, as Oskar Walzel reminds us, "this buffoonery was not a new note. . . ." Only, Walzel continues, "Tieck is mild and tame in comparison with Grabbe's mad ventures." ‡

---

* Heinrich von Kleist was also affected by the puppet theater of that time; witness his remarkable essay on that subject.
† This tradition, in turn, can be traced back to the Roman and Greek *mimus*, as Hermann Reich and others have shown. Martin Esslin claims its relation to the Theater of the Absurd in his book of that name, and points out how Grabbe belongs to that tradition. During the Enlightenment, Justus Möser, in his paper "Harlequin or the Defense of the Comic-Grotesque" (1761), dignified the Grotesque by according it a "category."
‡ Oskar Walzel, *German Romanticism*.

But what makes Grabbe's "mad ventures" effective is his genius for the stage and his ability to assimilate all these influences such that they emerge in a form that is uniquely his own. Indeed, it is the extraordinary fusion of the puppet/grotesque with the realistic/representational that gives *Jest* its great individuality as a work of dramatic literature. Prototypes can be found also of most of the characters in the play, but again to each Grabbe gives his special touch. Thus, the farcical take-off on the Schoolmaster may owe its origin to Wenzelaus in Lenz's *Der Hofmeister*, as well as to other tutors in German comedy, and to the *Dottore* figure of the *commedia dell'arte*. Similarly, Baron Murdrax may be traced to the *Capitano*; and Liddy may be likened to an aristocratic *Colombina*.

The portrait of the Devil naturally has many antecedents, especially in the popular folklore, and also in some of E. T. A. Hoffmann's stories, not to mention *Arlecchino*; but fortunately Grabbe added many original traits. Grabbe's is a somewhat secularized Devil, sharing the same emancipation from religious fires as Goethe's Mephistopheles. He even bears some of his author's personal characteristics. We can almost see the Devil in the description of Grabbe's ungainly person in Immermann's *Memoirs*: "Nothing in this body was in harmony. Fine and delicate—hands and feet so tiny that they seemed to me undeveloped—he moved with angular, rough, uncouth gestures; the arms did not know what the hands were doing, often the upper body and the feet were in opposition. These contrasts reached their apex in his face."

Grabbe also liked to think of himself as the Devil; in his letters, he frequently called himself Satan, and he took malicious glee in writing reviews of his own plays, commenting "Of course, Mephisto is hidden there in my letters to the magazine editors!" The Devil is certainly the pivotal character of the play. But we find some of Grabbe, or his experience, in every character—even in little Gottlieb.

In *Jest*, then, Grabbe used the edged tools inherited from the

Comedy of the Grotesque—jest,* satire, irony, plus wit, parody, scorn and sarcasm, punning and farce, scatology, and sometimes plain cruel slapstick. All this was further heightened by his own inclination toward comic self-portrayal and his talent for mischief and tomfoolery.

In a hostile climate, notes Walter Sokel, "comedy either changes into biting parody, of which German literature shows numerous excellent examples from Lenz and Büchner to Brecht, or drowns in pathos." † There is no pathos here except mock pathos; indeed, by the end of the play the laceration reaches such a point that, as Grabbe put it in another of his letters, "nothing in literature or life remains intact." In *Jest* all relationships are destroyed, the *modus vivendi* of the times drastically challenged, the fortresses of Romanticism demolished, and finally the *Ich* itself is dethroned—but all seemingly in fun, all somewhat tongue-in-cheek. When the Devil breaks the best chair in the house—*that* is Chaos. The good, holy object ends in ruins in the fireplace.

With most of the Romantics, the *Ich* remains the castle from which they spew aspersions out on the world. For Grabbe that was not enough: he does not spare *himself*. That is perhaps the deeper significance of the curious ending where all's well that ends well—or so it seems—until the author himself steps onto the stage, lantern in hand, and is called every name imaginable by the furiously jealous Schoolmaster who does not want to let him in. But he is already "in"—anticipating that great passage from Grabbe's *Hannibal*: "Yes, we won't fall out of this world. We're already in." ‡

---

* Thus the word *Scherz*, which I have translated as "Jest," implies "joke," "play," "farce." Allardyce Nicoll in his *History of World Drama* calls this same play "*Farce*, Satire, Irony and Deeper Meaning." Elsewhere it has been called "*Joke*, Satire, Irony," while Barbara Wright uses "*Comedy*, Satire, Irony." I chose "Jest" because it brings out the "playful" aspect of *Scherz*, at the same time also carrying the *joker* implication.
† Walter Sokel, *The Writer in Extremis*.
‡ "*Ja, aus der Welt werden wir nicht fallen. Wir sind einmal darin*," quoted by Freud in *Civilization and Its Discontents*. Cf. Heidegger's concept that we are "thrown" into Time.

In *Jest*, this scorn for all things, while Romantic in origin, becomes almost Nietzschean in scope—just as in *Gothland* despair becomes preexistential. Such an onslaught leads to a kind of comic nihilism—a mocking contempt for all standards, ethics, religion. Not even science and philosophy are spared, as witness the Natural Scientists in the first act when they examine the freezing Devil and conclude he is a German female-writer; or the "dark" tribute to Aristotle and Kant in Act II.

In *Gothland*, all that was left to believe in was *Time*. In *Jest*, even that is challenged, as in the Schoolmaster's premonition of relativity in the first scene of the play when he discusses the running time of a horse which does the final stretch "in quarter of an hour, in ten minutes, in one minute, in zero minutes, in no time at all, and finally in less than no time at all!" Or "Ypsilanti's disintegrating army" that "won a great battle on the 25th of *next* month."

Grabbe's nihilism takes on many other forms in the play. For example, with the comparatively lesser figure of the poet, Ratbane,* he is not simply mocking the conventional image of the poet: he is challenging the idea that the poet can achieve any true autonomy in life. But he cannot run away either. So that when Ratbane faces a true-life dilemma, he can do nothing—his teeth simply chatter. When Liddy says with smiling scorn, "Ratbane, you are a frightful coward!," all he can say in reply is: "I am a poet, dear lady!"

Liddy is an ironic phenomenon in herself. Throughout the play Grabbe pokes fun at women, especially that extravagant Biedermeier ideal of femininity, pointing out that the female usually has no brains, and if she does happen to, it is a mistake; that "feeling ruins the complexion" and "imagination causes

---

* *Rattengift*, in German = Ratbane, in English, or Ratpoison, Rough-on-Rats, etc. Thought by some commentators to be a take-off on Heine, who had just written his poetic tragedy, *Ratcliff*. But then, again, Ratbane may be simply an addition to Grabbe's menagerie of animals—the imagery of *Gothland* abounds in them.

blue rings under the eyes," and so forth—these barbs when all the while Liddy stands as a living contradiction to his argument. She may be a lady, but she's certainly outspoken! But Grabbe mocks not only the fragile, ultra-dainty lady and the rapacious lady-reader. He pours even more scorn on what he terms that monstrous "gargoyle," the German female-writer who floods the market with products of her literary fertility instead of staying at home, keeping house, and producing good little German babies.

As a matter of fact, Grabbe's sharp eye took in everything—not just literary and philosophic epiphenomena. He makes the folly of the upper classes and the feudalistic nobility look as ridiculous as the stupidity of the peasants and the workers; he travesties the night life of the big cities as much as he mockingly apostrophizes the verdant villages; and he exposes the limitations of the great moral philosophers as ruthlessly as he does the homilies of the country pastor. In fact, all society at the time of the Holy Alliance was hell, as Grabbe saw it! *

Then he turns against man himself as a creature. Having attacked him through his institutions, professions, and mores, he now stabs at the inner man. In sober circumstances, man has, he assumes, an apparent sense of values; he takes himself seriously and wants to be taken seriously by others. But lo, as Grabbe shows in the hilarious carousal scene (Act III, Scene 1), under the effect of drink, the mask falls off and man's true face is seen—*"im Wein ist Wahrheit."* Yet the vision is not appalling, and the stabs are now in fun: Ratbane sees himself as a mincing, contemptible worm; Mushcliff, in his drunken stupor, mistakes the Schoolmaster for Liddy and embraces him; the Schoolmaster, in turn, sees his father in little Gottlieb; while little Gottlieb, who now has a chance to hit back at his tyrannical master, climbs up on the numb tutor and pummels him

---

* Grabbe's unmasking of society is so thorough that it has lead to some interesting Marxist interpretations of this play. But Grabbe had no use for radicals of either the Right or the Left. He was a true iconoclast.

mercilessly. The crowning glory of this wild orgy of drink and psychic unbuttoning—a scene so well conceived and executed it must have been inspired by some of Grabbe's own student drinking bouts in Leipzig or Berlin—is the survivors' waddling off to church in pitch-black night to play the organ.

For obviously nothing was sacred to Grabbe; his scornful parody knew no bounds. Where does all this destructiveness end? "No man, least of all a productive man, can live on pure negation," wrote Stresau, one of Grabbe's most sympathetic commentators, musing upon the comedy. Still, is it pure negation when one can laugh at it all? But what had led young Grabbe to such depths? What fostered the deep despair of *Gothland* and the all-embracing cynicism of *Jest*?

It is tempting to assume that Grabbe must have undergone some shattering experience before or during the composition of these two plays, but there is no real evidence to support such a hypothesis. Is it not safer to recognize that Grabbe, along with other highly sensitive writers of this difficult transition period—Lenau, who committed suicide, Hölderlin, who went mad, Lermontov, Leopardi, Musset—came to maturity in the face of violently changing values? The revolution in thought alone was enough to unsettle young Kleist, who went into a tremendous state of depression after reading Kant, tore up the play he was working on at the time, and wrote to a friend: "My only and highest aim has sunk, and I have nothing left!" Nor can we underestimate the convulsive effect of the Romantics' discovery of the unconscious, and their obsession with the dark side of Nature.

While Grabbe was too solidly rooted in reality to fall into the solipsism of a Fichte and those writers most influenced by him, or to take the mystical path of a Novalis, such thoughts were nonetheless in the air; and it is not a far step from a mystical Kingdom-of-Being, identified with a Kingdom-of-Nothingness, to a harsh denial of all this folderol, and a leap into total nihilism.

If the descent into the depths of the unconscious and the exploration of the dark side of Nature represent to the Romantics a return to the lost world, to Rimbaud's real life which is "elsewhere," does it not follow that Gothland's nihilistic monologues and the Devil's divagations on the essence of this world might well represent Grabbe's *via dolorosa/via gioisa* to the meaning of existence?* But where the Romantics got lost in the unutterable, and had a dangerous incapacity to accept the real world (an incapacity also of self-acceptance), we never find Grabbe losing hold of reality or of himself. That is why his ability to laugh at the entire human lot in *Jest* is so exhilarating. As Ionesco, a modern master of the absurd, maintains: "The comic alone is able to give us the strength to bear the tragedy of existence."

For we must never forget this: *Jest* is still preeminently a comedy. The "deeper significance" neither defeats the fun nor damages the joy of the play. On the contrary, it seems to heighten the humor by giving it an extra dimension.

Indeed, it is the constant interplay of amusing paradox † that constitutes the real action of the play—not the fairly obvious, though pleasantly convenient, plot and subplots with their overlapping intrigues. We are amused at little Gottlieb being treated as if he were a genius, just as we are startled to hear the Schoolmaster discuss current events with the peasant Tobias. Devils do not usually appear wearing fur coats in the dog-day heat of August; while people who wear fur coats at that time of year do not ordinarily freeze—though devils may. The Devil's transgressions of the laws of physics are calmly noted down by the near-sighted Natural Scientists who do not leave until they are

---

* Cf. Nietzsche's: "We must experience nihilism before we can find out what values these 'values' really had.—We require, at some time, new values. . . ."
† Cf. Wilhelm Schlegel: "Romantic irony is identical with paradox." Hermann Reich points out in *Mimus* that "in a gloss to Juvenal, the mimes are called *paradoxi*."

thrown out—not, to be sure, by the Baron, their host, but by the Devil, a fellow guest. The Devil weeps over the performance of a noble deed; rich Liddy gives money for the village poor; ugly Mushcliff tickles the fancy of lovely Liddy; the "intellectual" Schoolmaster becomes a man of action after an all-night drinking bout. Paradox caps paradox. Good triumphs over evil; but evil is a farce. We even "keep laughing at a murderer until finally he laughs at himself for having taken the trouble to kill someone," opines the Devil, anticipating Musil's *Man without Qualities* in our century.

By endowing the play with multifaceted surfaces and potential meanings, Grabbe avoided the dilemma of total skepticism. Thus Liddy, the emancipated lady from the castle, and Mushcliff, the unspeakably ugly freeman, are relatively positive people. So they are treated with a gentle irony rather than the corrosive scorn that is poured on the other characters. In fact, their unsentimental engagement, or mésalliance, at the end lends an almost democratic accent to the play. Even the Baron —that harsh, gruff caricature of feudal obtuseness—much as we dislike him and his dogged conservatism, certainly copes with reality in a way that is equally hard to reconcile with a philosophy of despair. Indeed, all the characters of the play, including the bloody Baron Murdrax, that great take-off on the Junker type, are ultimately justified by their vitality.

Finally, a study could be made in terms of the ratio of reality to grotesquerie in each character, and the significance that bears on the philosophic action of the play as a whole. Even the most stable of Grabbe's personages is something of a contradiction, especially in terms of the society and literature the author wishes to ridicule—the exceptionally modest Mushcliff is most obviously so, being physically the antithesis of the hero of the period. And Liddy, however real and sympathetic, is unreal to her society just because she is so sensible and lovable: she is exactly what no other romantic heroine of that time dared to be. She is a paradox, too, in her wit and charm—a rare combination. As for the Baron, he is the height of contradiction;

for, in spite of his rantings, his intolerant tirades, he indulges Liddy her every whim, and takes her whole incredible menage of drunks, freethinkers, and versifiers under his wing. He even accepts the Devil as his guest.

Jest is both critic-proof and easily assailable: again a paradox. Heine, with every reason to dislike Grabbe (who is said to have attacked Heine once in Berlin), praised *Jest*. Though most other contemporaries called the work unplayable, time has proved otherwise. *Jest* was like a fresh gust of wind in its time: it still is. And it plays!

JEST, SATIRE, IRONY
AND DEEPER SIGNIFICANCE

CHARACTERS

Baron von Haldungen
Miss Liddy, his niece
Sir Wattsdale, her fiancé
Baron Murdrax
Mr. Mushcliff
Ratbane, a poet
The Village Schoolmaster
Tobias, a farmer
Little Gottlieb, his son
Gretchen, maidservant of the magistrate's wife
Konrad, the blacksmith
Four Natural Scientists
The Devil
His Grandmother
Emperor Nero, her servant
Grabbe, author of the comedy

Thirteen Apprentice Tailors,
   and other secondary characters

The scene is laid in and near the Baron's village.

ACT ONE

SCENE 1

The Schoolmaster's Room

SCHOOLMASTER *(seated at his table, pouring one drink after another from a large bottle):* —Schnapps with sugar!—*utile cum dulci!*—the useful with the sweet!—Today's going to be a tough grind—trying to teach the first declension to those yokels. A country oaf and the first declension! Just about as bad, it seems to me, as a crow trying to put on a starched dickie! *(He looks out the window.)* Confound it, here comes bow-legged Tobias with that half-wit son of his! Hang it all, where can I hide the schnapps?—Quick, I'll bury it in my stomach! *(He drains the bottle with horrifying rapidity.)* Ah, of such a mouthful Pestalozzi himself need not have been ashamed! Out the window with you! *(He tosses the empty bottle out the window.)*

(Enter Tobias and Little Gottlieb.)

TOBIAS: Hope you slept well, Mr. Schoolmaster.
SCHOOLMASTER: Thanks, cousin, thanks!—And how's the family?
TOBIAS: Oh, so so! The wife's healthy enough, but my prize pig's on its last legs. It moans and groans like an old man.
SCHOOLMASTER: A pity, a pity—as much for the pig as for the old man.
TOBIAS: Well, what's new on the political horizon, Mr. Schoolmaster? What do the latest papers say? Have the Greeks won? Have they driven out their traditional enemy—the Turks?

SCHOOLMASTER: The stars are not unfavorable. The *Hamburg Non-Partisan* has slaughtered another thirty thousand Turks, and the *Nüremberg Correspondent* continues untiringly to rape virgins of the noblest Greek families; while it is also being whispered about—and this from the most dependable sources—that Ypsilanti's disintegrating army won a great battle on the 25th of next month.

TOBIAS *(mouth agape)*: On the 25th of *next*—?

SCHOOLMASTER: Don't look so amazed, Tobias! The couriers are fast nowadays! Improved post roads, improved post roads!

TOBIAS: So help me God! Such a post road—where the courier runs ahead of the news by one month—I'd sure like to see that once before I die!

SCHOOLMASTER: Frankly, something like that is rare around here. But certainly in your own experience, Tobias, you must have observed that a good horse on a good road cuts down an hour's run to half an hour. Now, if you can imagine an even better horse and even finer roads *ad infinitum*, then you naturally reach the point where the horse does the stretch in quarter of an hour, in ten minutes, in one minute, in zero minutes, in no time at all, and finally in less than no time at all! Do you get it?

TOBIAS: I get it; but the Devil get me, I still don't understand it!

SCHOOLMASTER: Since you already get it, it doesn't much matter whether you also understand it. Still, as Cicero said to Caesar—oh, oh, what's that you're pulling out of your pocket?

TOBIAS: Well, that's just why I brought little Gottlieb along to call on you. My wife sends you her compliments, and begs most kindly if you can make do with this sausage.

SCHOOLMASTER: Make do with it? *(He grabs the sausage and gobbles it down.)*

TOBIAS: You see, our little Gottlieb's got the worms, and so his mother thinks that some day we might make a scholar of him. Isn't that right, little Gottlieb? Don't you want to be a scholar?

ACT ONE, SCENE 1

LITTLE GOTTLIEB: Yes, I have worms.

SCHOOLMASTER: My good fellow, you may rest assured that I know how to assess the manifold talents of your most promising son.

TOBIAS: Now my wife and I would like you to take the boy into your home, and, with all due respect, make a minister of him. It would do us proud to see him, with all due respect, standing in the pulpit! And to show how much we appreciate all this, every St. Martin's Day we want to send you nine fat geese and a kegful of schnapps.

SCHOOLMASTER: What? A kegful? And filled to the brim?

TOBIAS: Burping full, Mr. Schoolmaster!

SCHOOLMASTER: Every inch a schnapps! You can already count your son among the intelligentsia! I shall not only initiate him into the deepest mysteries of dogmatics, homiletics, and other related sciences of theology, but shall also see to it that he is instructed in the major plastic, idyllic, and mephytic * sciences of our country ministers, as, for instance, the sciences of pork-chopping, cattle-slaughtering, and dung-loading. And, in order to show you how close to my heart I hold little Gottlieb and his welfare, I shall betake myself with him up to the castle this very day. There I shall present him as a genius to the young Baroness and her uncle, who arrived only yesterday. Perhaps he will be deemed worthy of extra-special subsidy for his studies.

TOBIAS: Now do that, Mr. Schoolmaster, do! But I beg you, don't overstuff the boy with learning. I've got a pair of oxen that pull with their heads, so I know what hard work headwork is! Good morning to you! *(Exits.)*

SCHOOLMASTER *(to Little Gottlieb)*: Now come here, you little fool, and pay attention! I'm going to tell you what you have to do up at the castle to look like a genius: either you must

---

* mephytic: derived from the name of an old Italian goddess, venerated as protector against poisonous vapors, sulphuric fumes, etc. Hence, stinking, fetid, foul.

never open your mouth—then they'll think: Confound it, he must have a lot to hide, for he doesn't say a word. Or you must say something absolutely nonsensical—then they'll think: Confound it, he must have said something very profound, for we, who understand everything else, didn't understand a word of this. Or you must eat spiders and swallow flies—then they'll think: Confound it all, there's a big man for you (or, rather, as you should more appropriately be called, a big boy), for neither flies nor spiders nauseate him. So tell me, stupid, which do you want to do?

LITTLE GOTTLIEB: I want to keep my mouth shut.

SCHOOLMASTER: Well, shut up then, and as far as I'm concerned, keep it shut—with your hand glued to your mouth, for that looks even more allegorical and poetical. However, all that notwithstanding, I can't let you off without instructing you in another very indispensable prerequisite: you must occasionally show a geniuslike absent-mindedness. Which you do more or less like this, little Gottlieb: before leaving the house, you stick a dead cat in your watchpocket; later on, you take a stroll in the evening dusk with a beautiful young lady. While gazing up at the stars, all of a sudden you pull out the dead cat and hold it up to your nose as if you wanted to blow into it, whereupon the lady, pale as death, shrieks, "Holy cats, a dead cat!" You, however, answer distractedly, "Oh, Lord, I thought it was a star!" Something like that gives you a reputation for originality, you abortion! *(He gives him a box on the ear.)*

LITTLE GOTTLIEB: Ow! Ow! Ow!

SCHOOLMASTER: Don't be scared, little Gottlieb! *Utile cum dulci*, the useful with the sweet—an *ear*, because it's useful; a *box* of candy because it's sweet; thus a *box* on the *ear*. It is one of the niceties of my educational methods, I'll have you know, that with every interesting precept, I give the pupil a tooth-rattling slap in the face. Then ever afterward, whenever he recalls the slap, he will also remember the lesson it accompanied.... So, *allons*, to the castle! Dip the pen deep into the inkwell and draw a thick dark line right smack across my nose and face! For even upon my countenance, let my gracious masters perceive the traces of my diligence! *(Little Gottlieb draws a thick line across his face, and both exit.)*

SCENE 2

*Bright, warm summer day.
The Devil sits on a hill and freezes.*

DEVIL: 'Tis cold . . . cold. 'Tis much warmer in Hell!—Just because the number seven appears most frequently in the Bible, satirical grandmother had me wear seven fur shirtlets, seven fur jacketkins, and seven fur cappies—but still 'tis cold . . . cold—God fetch my soul, but it's cold!—If I could only steal some wood or set a forest on fire—set a forest on fire!—Oh, by all the angels, that *would* be something all right if the Devil froze to death!—Steal wood . . . burn forest . . . burn . . . steal. . . . *(He freezes to death.)*

(Enter a Natural Scientist, botanizing.)

A NATURAL SCIENTIST: Truly, there is rare vegetation to be found in this region: Linnaeus, Jussieu—Lord Christ, what's this lying here on the ground? A dead man, and as one can clearly see, frozen to death! Now, that *is* peculiar. A miracle, if there really be such a thing as a miracle! We note down that today, the second of August, the sun stands flaming in heaven; it is the hottest day I've ever experienced; and this man here, against all laws and observations of learned men, dares to, presumes to freeze himself to death!—No, it's impossible! Absolutely impossible! I shall have to put on my glasses! *(He puts on his glasses.)* Extraordinary! Extraordinary! Here, I've put on my glasses, and the fellow is nonetheless frozen. Highly extraordinary! I shall take him to my colleagues. *(He grabs the Devil by the collar and drags him away.)*

SCENE 3

A Room in the Castle

The Devil lies on the table with four Natural Scientists standing around him.

FIRST NATURAL SCIENTIST: You will concede, Gentlemen, that this dead being here presents itself as a most complicated case.

SECOND NATURAL SCIENTIST: That depends upon your point of view! It is a shame, though, his fur clothes are so labyrinthically buttoned together that that world circumnavigator Captain Cook himself could not unbutton them.

FIRST NATURAL SCIENTIST: You will concede it is a man?

THIRD NATURAL SCIENTIST: Certainly! It has five fingers and no tail.

FOURTH NATURAL SCIENTIST: The only question to be resolved, then, is this: What kind of man is it?

FIRST NATURAL SCIENTIST: Precisely! But here one cannot proceed cautiously enough, and, although it is broad daylight, I would advise that a light be added.

THIRD NATURAL SCIENTIST: Quite right, dear colleague!
(They light a candle and set it on the table near the Devil.)

FIRST NATURAL SCIENTIST *(after all four have examined the Devil with the most exacting attention)*: Gentlemen, I now feel clear as to the identity of this puzzling cadaver, and I trust I do not err. Note this turned-up nose, these big, thick boastful lips—note, I say the inimitable trait of godlike coarseness spread over the entire countenance, and indubitably you will see lying before you one of our present-day critics, indeed a genuine specimen.

SECOND NATURAL SCIENTIST: My dear colleague, I cannot fully agree with your opinion, extraordinarily perspicacious as it may be. Not to mention that our modern reviewers, especially the critics of drama, are more foolish than they are coarse; and so I perceive on this dead face not a single one of those characteristics you have just chosen to enumerate for us. I discern, on the contrary, something positively maidenlike there: the bushy, overhanging eyebrows hint at that delicate, female modesty which tries to conceal even its own glances; and the nose, which you call turned-up, seems rather to have been tilted back, out of politeness, to leave an extra-large open expanse upon which the languishing lover might lavish his kisses—but enough. If I am not deceived, this frozen person is, indeed, a parson's daughter.

THIRD NATURAL SCIENTIST: I must confess, Sir, that your hypothesis strikes me as somewhat bold. I conjecture it to be the Devil.

FIRST and SECOND NATURAL SCIENTISTS: But that is, *ab initio*, impossible, for the Devil does not fit into our system.

FOURTH NATURAL SCIENTIST: Esteemed colleagues, let us not wrangle! Now I shall give you *my* opinion, with which I wager you will immediately concur. Observe the monstrous ugliness screaming out at us from every feature of this face, and you cannot help but concede that, were there no German female writers, such a gargoyle would be inconceivable.

THE THREE OTHER NATURAL SCIENTISTS: Yes, it is a German female writer. We yield to your more weighty arguments.

FOURTH NATURAL SCIENTIST: I thank you, my colleagues!—But what is this? Observe how, since we set the burning candle before its nose, the corpse begins to stir? Now the fingers twitch, now her head trembles, she opens her eyes, she's alive!

DEVIL *(raising himself upright on the table)*: Where . . . where am I?—Ugh, I'm still freezing! *(To the Natural Scientists)*

Please, Gentlemen, shut both those windows—I can't stand drafts.

FIRST NATURAL SCIENTIST *(while he closes the windows)*: You must have weak lungs.

DEVIL *(while he climbs down from the table)*: Not always! Not when I'm sitting in a well-heated oven.

SECOND NATURAL SCIENTIST: What? You sit in well-heated ovens?

DEVIL: I make a habit of doing so, every now and then.

THIRD NATURAL SCIENTIST: Remarkable addiction! *(Writes it down.)*

FOURTH NATURAL SCIENTIST: You're an authoress, Madam, are you not?

DEVIL: An authoress? What do you mean? Such women are plagued by the Devil, but God preserve the Devil they be the Devil themselves?

ALL FOUR SCIENTISTS: What? So then { it *is* / you *are* / he *is* / she *is* } the Devil?

(They start to run off.)

DEVIL *(aside)*: Aha! Now for once I can lie to my heart's content. *(Aloud)* Gentlemen! Gentlemen! Where are you going? Be calm! Relax! Surely you're not running away from some mere play on my name, are you? *(The Natural Scientists turn back.)* They *call* me the Devil, but that's not who I really *am*.

FIRST NATURAL SCIENTIST: With whom, then, have we the honor of speaking?

DEVIL: With Theophilus Christian Devil, Bishop in the Duchy of _____'s service, Honorary Member of a Society for the Advancement of Christianity among the Jews, and Knight of the Papal Order for Civil Merit, recently—in the Middle Ages—bestowed upon me by the Pope for keeping the rabble in a state of perpetual fear.

ACT ONE, SCENE 3

FOURTH NATURAL SCIENTIST: Which means you must indeed have reached a ripe old age by now.

DEVIL: You err: I am only eleven years old.

THIRD NATURAL SCIENTIST *(to the second)*: The biggest fibber I've ever met!

SECOND NATURAL SCIENTIST *(to the third)*: And so will he please the ladies very, very much!

(The Devil has been getting closer and closer to the candle, and has involuntarily stuck his finger into the flame.)

FIRST NATURAL SCIENTIST: Good Lord, Bishop, what are you doing? Why, you're holding your finger in the fire!

DEVIL *(embarrassed, withdrawing the finger)*: I—I love it, I love to hold my finger in a flame.

THIRD NATURAL SCIENTIST: Peculiar passion! *(Makes a note of it.)*

(Enter Baron von Haldungen, Liddy, Wattsdale, and Ratbane.)

FOURTH NATURAL SCIENTIST. Ah, the Baron and his guests.

FIRST NATURAL SCIENTIST *(to the newcomers)*: Let me herewith present you Bishop Theophilus Devil, who in the Middle Ages became a Knight of the Papal Order for Civil Merit, and who is not only accustomed to sitting in well-heated ovens, but also likes to stick his finger into a flame.

RATBANE: Why, Bishop, you come as though called upon to unite the fair Liddy and Sir Wattsdale.

DEVIL *(embarrassed)*: To couple them? I? *(Half-aloud)* Holy Mary, I don't know the text.

LIDDY: Don't curse so, Bishop! There are a couple of months yet before the coupling!

WATTSDALE: Liddy, how can you so long deny me this hand which I, so full of longing, press to my lips?

LIDDY *(indignantly pulling away her hand)*: Sir Wattsdale, please! I don't relish such foolery.

WATTSDALE: O my dearest lady, my devotion to you is so boundless that I—

BARON: A pinch of snuff, Sir Wattsdale? *(Wattsdale takes it and sneezes violently.)*

(Meanwhile the Devil has turned back to the flame and once again holds his finger in it.)

THE FOUR SCIENTISTS *(who have followed his every movement, call out)*: Look, look, Gentlemen, the Bishop has his finger in the flame again!

DEVIL: Oh, there I go again—*(He tears off his left arm with his right hand, and thrashes the Natural Scientists out of the room with it; whereupon he sets the arm back on and returns to the party.)*

RATBANE: Sir! Sir! How I marvel at you! You rip out your arm and set it back on again as if taking off and putting on a stocking! Truly, that would be too audacious even in poetry—how much more so in real life!

DEVIL: You work yourself up over nothing! Simple sleight-of-hand! I studied theology in the University of ———— where you can pick up any number of such parlor tricks on the side!

(Enter a servant.)

SERVANT: The Schoolmaster wishes to be admitted. He has with him a young genius whom he would like to present to Your Lordship and his guests.

BARON: Tell that old drunken schoolmaster he and that genius of his can go hang themselves!

LIDDY: Ah, Uncle dear, don't spoil our fun! The Schoolmaster is the drollest eccentric I know. And yet in the midst of all his tomfoolery, he still knows very well what he's about. Most likely he's fished up some terribly stupid village lout whom he will introduce to us as a great poet, and quite brazenly compare him to Homer and Ariosto.

BARON: All right, show them in. *(Exit Servant.)* And you, Bishop, you must put the screws on him!

DEVIL: I'll make him squirm, Baron!

WATTSDALE *(to Liddy)*: But you are always the one to whom—

ACT ONE, SCENE 3

BARON: A pinch of snuff, Sir Wattsdale. (*Wattsdale takes it and sneezes.*)
LIDDY: The Schoolmaster has probably received another shipment of fresh herring, Mr. Ratbane.
RATBANE: Those confounded herrings! (*Exits, fuming.*)
BARON: What's this about herrings, my spiteful, gleeful niece? They seem to have annoyed Ratbane considerably.
LIDDY: Patience, Uncle darling! You will find out any minute now—straight from the Schoolmaster's mouth.

(*Enter the Schoolmaster and Little Gottlieb.*)

SCHOOLMASTER (*with deep bows*): My greatest respects and—
WATTSDALE: Good heavens, Schoolmaster, what's that frightful inkstain doing all over your face?
SCHOOLMASTER (*pretending astonishment*): I—an inkstain—really?—Ah, Your Grace, now you can see for yourself with what diligence—with what zeal—
LIDDY: Don't put yourself out so, Mr. Schoolmaster! We know what something like that means to you, don't we? Yesterday, while the sun was setting, a great idea dawned upon you, and, as you didn't happen to have any blank paper on you just then, in the haste of the moment you simply had to jot it down on your face!
SCHOOLMASTER: Not a bad guess, my dear young lady—
LIDDY: Or else by chance you saw yourself in the mirror, and, your face striking you as too impossible, you blotted it out!
SCHOOLMASTER: You become cruel, Miss Liddy, cruel! Ink is the true lifeblood of a scholar, and woe to the scholar whose lifeblood sits on his face, for it looks very ugly and makes black spots.
BARON and WATTSDALE: A mad pedant.
LIDDY (*softly to the Schoolmaster*): All joking aside, did old Mary get the money?
SCHOOLMASTER: Yes, gracious Miss, and she wept for joy—
LIDDY: Hush! Here's another *louis d'or* for her—tell her I shall visit her this evening.

(Devil, who in the meantime has gradually approached the candle again, begins suddenly to weep and sob loudly.)

BARON: Hello there, what's got into the Bishop all of a sudden? He's blubbering like a waterspout.

WATTSDALE: So he is: tears are streaming down his cheeks!

SCHOOLMASTER: A bishop?—little Gottlieb, make a nice bow!

LIDDY: What's bothering you, Sir?

DEVIL: Ach! How can you ask! Something noble must have taken place here!

BARON: Something noble?

SCHOOLMASTER: The Bishop's right. Just this minute Miss Liddy gave me a *louis d'or* for poor old Mary, who's ill.

DEVIL: You hear now, Gentlemen?

WATTSDALE: And that's why you began to cry?

DEVIL *(drying his eyes)*: Yes, it made me melancholy.

LIDDY: Now relax. It won't happen again for a while!

BARON: I don't know—in a bishop that's most singular indeed.

WATTSDALE: What do you make of this, Schoolmaster?

SCHOOLMASTER: Your Reverence seems most sentimental.

BARON: Sentimental? Where did you pick up that miserable word?

SCHOOLMASTER: In the *Journal for Elegant Society*.*

BARON: The *Journal for Elegant Society*? And where did you pick up that?

LIDDY: Now, Uncle dear, remember the herrings esthetic Ratbane ran away from?

SCHOOLMASTER: Yes, Baron, and thereby hangs a tale. I have a rather distant cousin in town—a Mr. Pennysucker—who runs a not unprofitable business in packing wire, gems, copperplate, fish, and secondhand trousers.

BARON: We can believe it.

SCHOOLMASTER: Every two weeks this man sends me a small

---

* The *Journal for Elegant Society* (*Zeitung für die elegante Welt*) was a widely circulated and influential magazine of belles-lettres (1801–1852).

package of half-spoiled herring, for which I pay the ludicrously low price of fourteen groschen. Each herring, however, he wraps up individually, and very carefully, in fresh proofsheets, usually of the most miserable poetic works and magazines. This way I am kept rather well posted on the better products of our contemporary literature.

BARON: Ha ha ha! A herring literature!

SCHOOLMASTER: It is thus I receive the poetry of August Kuhn,* the *Tales* of Krug von Nidda,† the *Jew's Harp or Lyre-Tones* by Theodor Hell, ‡ and the *Tragedies* of a certain Mr. Houwald.**

WATTSDALE: By Jove, those are all famous writers for women, each one a ladies' favorite.

LIDDY: Sir Wattsdale, if, as now seems to be the fashion, one calls the dullest writers ladies' favorites, one deals us a really poor compliment.

BARON: Child, don't blame Sir Wattsdale! Think! Houwald, the tender, soulful Houwald! Wrapped around a herring! What an insult!

SCHOOLMASTER: Not an insult, Baron. Rather, an improvement! This good man likes to be satirical, too, upon occasion! Thus for some time now he has been trying to write a parody on *Guilt*,†† which, with all its faults, has still, I feel, a quality

---

* August Kuhn (1784–1829), Berlin teacher, scholar, poet, and novelist. Coeditor, with Kotzebue, of *Der Freimütige*, which Grabbe mocks later in the play.
† Friedrich Albrecht Franz Krug von Nidda (1776–1843), soldier-writer and professor of history in Leipzig, where Grabbe heard him lecture.
‡ Theodor Hell (pseudonym of Karl Gottfried Theodor Winkler, 1775–1856), Dresden writer and influential personality in the pseudoromantic Dresden "Liederkreis." Publisher of the *Abendzeitung*, for which Grabbe wrote his Detmold theater letters in 1828.
** Christoph Ernst, Freiherr von Houwald (1778–1845), tragedian. Author of successful Fate tragedies *Das Bild* and *Der Leuchturm*, he later parodied Müllner's *Schuld*.
†† *Guilt* (*Die Schuld*), here subject to Grabbe's mockery, was by Amadeus Gottfried Adolf Müllner (1774–1829), and one of the best known Fate tragedies.

that is well beyond your critics' comprehension. His mighty concoction is called, so I am led to believe, *The Fly-swatter*,* and contains much triviality, but not a grain of salt. Since, however, my wrapped herrings have taken pity upon it, it has become salty through and through, so that even Müllner,† were he to put it to his mouth, would exclaim: "Never before have I tasted anything so salty!"

BARON: *Bravissimo*, Mr. Schoolmaster, you are my man! But how on earth, stuck out there in the village, do you hit upon these sarcastic views on our modern writing?

SCHOOLMASTER *(bowing before Liddy)*: Here stands my teacher. When Miss Liddy was sick last winter, every evening I had to read aloud from the most recently published works: I profited no little from that experience, especially as she condemned most of them to the fire.

LIDDY: The Schoolmaster does me too great an honor.

(During this conversation the Devil has sneaked off to the side. Grinning maliciously, he has broken a chair, stuck the pieces in the fireplace, taken out his chemical lighter, set the wood on fire, pulled out a folding screen, and retired behind it.)

WATTSDALE *(who misses him first)*: But where is our bishop?

BARON: He seems to have slipped away. Very likely he's another one of those new scribblers.

SCHOOLMASTER: Yes, yes, probably he, too, will be wrapped around a putrid herring.

BARON *(angrily)*: They should wrap the whole Leipzig Book Fair around putrid herrings! Young Jewboys, whose education consists of nothing but eating pork, presume to set themselves up on the critics' night stools, and not only praise the most wretched poetic quacks to the stars, but even insult honorable men with their eulogies *(Liddy turns sharply away*

---

* Reference to *The Fly-swatter* (*Die Fliegenklatsche*) has to do with Houwald's satire of *Die Schuld*, in which a fly-swatter figures fatally.
† Müllner, author of *Guilt*. See note above.

ACT ONE, SCENE 3

at the first vulgar expressions, and talks eagerly with Wattsdale, pretending not to hear what the Baron says. The Baron carries on all the more violently.) Rhymesters, so stupid that every time one of their pieces reaches the public the price of asses is jacked up, are called "excellent poets." Actors, so boring everyone applauds with joy when they finally retire, are called "distinguished artists." Old hags, who sing so shrilly one could cut a slice of bread with their voices, are called "born dramatic singers"! The Tragic Muse has turned into a streetwalker whom every scoundrel ravishes and from that union produces five-legged mooncalves so abominable I pity the dog that pisses on them! The words "ingenious, soulful, genial, splendid" are becoming so monstrously misused that already I see the day when carved upon the gallows of our most infamous escaped jailbreaker there'll be the inscription: "This man is ingenious, genial, splendid, and soulful." O that a powerful genius might arise at last, who, armored from head to foot with godly strength, shall take charge of the German Parnassus and drive the rabble back into the swamps from which it has crawled forth!!

SCHOOLMASTER: That genius has arisen, Baron, he stands before you. He is little Gottlieb.

LIDDY (*bursting out laughingly*): What an idea!

SCHOOLMASTER: He *is* a genius, Miss Liddy, he *is*! He threw his mother's soup bowl out the window!

LITTLE GOTTLIEB (*half-crying*): I—I—I—

SCHOOLMASTER: Look. Can you not see with what presence of mind he throws himself into a picturesque pose? How he scratches behind his ears? The exact stance of Hogarth's whining street urchin! I have maintained from the beginning that a great potential talent for the picture-play lies hidden in little Gottlieb.

BARON: Schoolmaster, what do you mean by "picture-play"?

SCHOOLMASTER: Picture-plays are something new, Baron. The child who likes to play with colors and little pictures is very happy to have invented them. Now the nature of the *picture-*

play is such that everything occurring in it is picturesque, so that, for example, the personages who appear in the paintings are always simpletons, as, among others, the Knight Nanni, Van Dyck, Spinarosa, the Duchess of Sorrento,* etc.

BARON: Well, Sir Wattsdale, what do you think of this explanation of picture-plays?

WATTSDALE: I fear the Schoolmaster finds them more picturesque than their creators would have liked.

LIDDY: I don't understand why, Gentlemen, but it's getting unusually close here in this room.

WATTSDALE *(who already has had to wipe his forehead several times)*: Yes, yes, I feel a growing heat. It almost seems as though a fire has been lit.

BARON: Don't be ridiculous! It's the sun glaring down upon the chimney.

LIDDY: Which of them is right, little Gottlieb?

LITTLE GOTTLIEB: Yes.

LIDDY: Oh dear, but he's a stupid numskull, Schoolmaster!

SCHOOLMASTER: A numskull genius, like so many to be found today. He needs to be understood—he has depth! Nor are his writings wrapped around rotten herrings!

LIDDY: That speaks in his favor. At least it proves he's written nothing yet.

WATTSDALE *(to the Baron)*: Don't you see the smoke that's filling the room? That couldn't possibly come from the sun!

BARON: I acknowledge my error—a fire hasn't broken out next door, has it?

DEVIL *(singing out from the fireplace behind the folding screen, to the tune of Goethe's "Fisherman Song")*:
        Ah, if only you knew how cosy it is
        For the Devil in the fire—*(He warbles.)*

---

* Van Dyck and the Knight Nanni are characters in *Van Dijk's Country Life* (*Van Dijks Landleben*), a drama by Johann Friedrich Kind (1768–1843). The painter Spinarosa and the Duchess of Sorrento figure in Houwald's *The Portrait* (*Das Bild*).

ACT ONE, SCENE 3

BARON: Why, of all things, that's the voice of the Knight of the Papal Order of Civil Merit!

SCHOOLMASTER (*who has run behind the folding screen and now emerges, horrified*): No, no, no! My hair's standing on end! The Bishop's sitting there in the middle of the blazing fireplace, swallowing live coals, and striking up his trills—may God have mercy upon us!

ALL: What!? (*They pull away the folding screen, whereupon the Devil is seen emerging from the fireplace.*)

SCHOOLMASTER: Do you see now how he climbs out? *O tempora, o mores!*

BARON (*to the Devil*): Dammit, Sir, what kind of behavior is this? Are you mad? To squat in the fireplace? To swallow live coals—

DEVIL (*aside*): Now is the time to be coarse and put on a bold front! (*To the Schoolmaster*) You low-down, stinking toad's snot-rag. How dare you maintain I was sitting in the fireplace?

SCHOOLMASTER: Sir—

DEVIL: Yes, now I am firmly convinced that the fifty bottomless barrels of Danaid were fifty schoolmasters, for everything else gets filled eventually—everything, that is, but such a drunken how-to-box-children's-ears specialist! How, I ask myself again, how could you, you befuddled schnapps-leech, see me sitting in the fireplace if you weren't blind drunk? I was just sitting in front of it, blowing the coals.

SCHOOLMASTER: What in the blazes, Bishop—

DEVIL: What? You still won't shut up, you—

LIDDY: Quiet! I've had enough of this insult and abuse.

BARON: Just tell us how you got the fire started!

DEVIL (*with obvious pleasure*): Why, with the lovely chair that was standing over there in the corner!

BARON: Really! With that lovely chair?—Liddy, what have you to say to *that*?

LIDDY: It was the best chair in the whole house!

DEVIL: Was it really? Just what I thought—my hunch was right! (*He gloats.*)

BARON: Should I have the rascal thrown in the doghouse?
WATTSDALE: I should have nothing against it.
LIDDY: Uncle, what *are* you thinking of? The man is just beginning to interest me! I beg you, let him have a room in the castle! I'll pay for whatever chairs he may break.
BARON: Oh, you women! How quickly you fall in love with madness! *(To the Devil)* If you would like to stay with us, Sir, you will find a charming room at your disposal.
DEVIL: I accept your most agreeable offer and thank you from the bottom—*(To himself)* What? Thanks. But gratitude is a virtue! *(Aloud)* I don't give a damn whether you offer me lodging or not! It is also highly imprudent, if not downright silly of you to take a total stranger into your house without checking up on him! Moreover, where is that low-down dog of a lackey who is to show me my room? *(Exits.)*
BARON: There, Niece, you have a guest who's brazen enough.
WATTSDALE: Why don't you say "*blazing enough*"!
BARON: And I fear, my dear, you shan't be able to stand him for even an hour.
LIDDY: Don't let that worry you.
BARON: He'll be sure to push his insolence to the extreme.
LIDDY: In that case, I'll have him thrown out of the castle.
BARON: Ah, you *do* know how to look after yourself when necessary!—Your arm! We'll take coffee down in the garden.
LIDDY: I'll be along in a minute.

(Exit the Baron and Wattsdale.)

LIDDY *(to the Schoolmaster)*: Here!—Here's something extra for that thirsty palate of yours. Now there, don't be ashamed, I know your old weakness. But get that *louis d'or* over to old Mary as fast as you can.
SCHOOLMASTER: Immediately, Your Ladyship!
LIDDY: Adieu. *(Exits.)*
SCHOOLMASTER: Divine creature!—And you, little Gottlieb, what about you? You've not been duly appreciated, you poor child! Console yourself, for it was the same with all the great

minds—Solon, Plato, Cartouche,* Robespierre, Henry IV, and Caligula. They, too, experienced this same sad fate!— Come! I'm going to lock you up for four days and give you nothing to eat. Perhaps that will make you even more meditative than you are already. (*Little Gottlieb screams; the Schoolmaster exits with him.*)

SCENE 4

Another Room in the Castle

(*Enter the Devil.*)

DEVIL: Just you wait, Baron! So you've given me a room in your castle—I'll get even with you yet!—Liddy wants to marry Wattsdale; so she gets a husband. I'll put a stop to that, or I'm not the Devil! Still, I don't understand what makes me so irritable! I feel so despondent—so touched, so nostalgic— God fetch me, but the horseshoe on my hoof must have come loose. (*While he tears loose the cloths wrapped about the foot and takes a look at his hoof*) Oh, oh! It's only too true! The shoeing is off, it's worn out! I can hardly bear to touch the floor! Oh, misery! Unfortunately there's nothing to be done but conquer these trepidations of mine and call in a blacksmith. (*He rewraps the bindings and then calls*) Service!

(*Enter a servant.*)

SERVANT: You called, Sir?

---

* Louis Dominique Cartouche (1693–1721), leader of a French band of robbers and murderers, often glorified by poets and painters for his courage.

DEVIL: Listen, my good man! Is there a blacksmith in the village?
SERVANT: There are two here, Your Grace.
DEVIL: Then go, my son, and fetch he who laughs least!
SERVANT: Oho, then I'd better get hold of Fat Konrad. He's become dreadfully sad again—ever since the old highway was repaired. *(Exits.)*
DEVIL: I—O, woe is me! Now, how in the world am I going to break the news gently to this blacksmith—that I've a cloven hoof? *(Groans.)* Woe is me! O, woe is me!—Ha, here he comes! Courage!

(Enter Blacksmith.)

BLACKSMITH: Your Reverence sent for me—
DEVIL: Are you the—the—
BLACKSMITH: —the village smithy. Where's the nag I'm supposed to shoe?
DEVIL *(heatedly)*: Sir, I'm no—*(Claps his hand over his mouth.)* Oh, what a fool am I! Take a seat, my dear Mr. Blacksmith, take a seat! Have you a wife?
BLACKSMITH: Indeed I have!
DEVIL: A worthy woman, no doubt!
BLACKSMITH *(sighing)*: Well now, we all have our weaknesses!
DEVIL *(likewise sighing)*: Yes, indeed we do!
BLACKSMITH *(standing up)*: If you would be kind enough to tell me—
DEVIL: Ah, you're in a hurry, a great hurry! Paterfamilias? Y'wear boots! Y'have feet! *(Playing with the buttons on his vest)* I, too—no, I don't have—horse-hooves!
BLACKSMITH: Why, I'm sure of that—even without looking, Your Reverence.
DEVIL *(with great zeal)*: Yes, you can be sure of that, even without looking—even *with* looking, Mr. Smithy! I don't have horse-hooves—none—at most only . . . *(Softly, while, with tremendous effort and violent sneezing, he brings forth the words "noble, moral, Christian," etc.)* Mr. Smithy, you are

ACT ONE, SCENE 4

an–an–igno–no–n–n–noble, mo–mo–moron — mo–mo–moral soul, a cultivated man, a religious, diligent, ch–church–ch–churchgoing Christian—I can confide in you (*While he tries to hide his right leg behind the left*) I have a hoof on my right foot!

BLACKSMITH (*with inquisitive glances*): How? What? A hoof? Ugh!

DEVIL: No, no, no! Not so much a hoof as a horse's foot—or, rather more exactly, a horselike—that is, a humanlike—well, in short, a somewhat thick sole, which from a distance, if one is short-sighted, might appear to be a horse's hoof.

BLACKSMITH (*stammering with curiosity*): If—if Your Grace would show me the—the sole of your—

DEVIL: Right away, my dear Blacksmith, right away!—But bolt the door first!—That's it! (*After loosening the cloths from his hoof, he shows it to the Blacksmith, and, ashamed, hides his face in his handkerchief.*) Now, if you would be so kind as to fit your shoe onto it!

BLACKSMITH (*taking the foot in his hand*): Listen, Mister, that's not the sole of a foot, it's a horse-hoof, the like of which in all Christendom not another nag—not another soul, I meant to say—can boast of!

DEVIL (*keeping his face in his handkerchief and lisping*): Shoe me! Shoe it on!

BLACKSMITH: Just by chance I've got a horseshoe as big as a chandelier, here in my bag. I'll shoe it on you in real style! (*He shoes it on him.*) There, now it fits fast.

DEVIL (*glad*): Does it fit?

BLACKSMITH: That'll be one gulden.

DEVIL (*to himself*): One gulden? I'd be a fool! (*Aloud*) Cheapskate! Have you any idea whom you've just shod? I am Satan himself, I am—(*The Blacksmith runs out, and the Devil calls out after him*) five hundred thousand years old and then some! I got your grandfather, and I hope to get you, too. If you so much as breathe a word about me, I'll wring your neck! And I should pay you! You ought to be hanged! Go hang yourself, you gallows-bird! *(Coming back)* How the old sinner tore out of here when he heard my real name! But I've got to hand it to him, he did me up right well! The horseshoe fits as if it had grown on! Ah, I feel all my powers returning! *(He paws the ground several times with his cloven hoof.)* Now I shall try to sleep for an hour or so to restore my faculties, and then foul up that wedding with redoubled zeal! *(He sits down in an armchair and pulls a book out of his pocket.)* Ah, it's a good thing I brought along that old, infallible sleeping pill—Klopstock's *Messiah*! I need read only three verses of it, and I'm tired as the devil! *(Opening the book)* Where did I leave off last time? Ah, page twenty-nine. *(He reads two verses to himself and falls asleep.)*

ACT TWO

SCENE 1

Hall in the Castle

(*Enter the Devil with rewrapped horse-hoof.*)

DEVIL: There's a giant of a fellow prowling about here whose long fingers seem to point perpetually to the gallows upon which he will ultimately hang! Perhaps he will fit into my plan!—Hush, there he comes! I'll step off to the side and listen in on what he has to say.

(*Enter Baron Murdrax.*)

MURDRAX: That Liddy's a magnificent animal, and suits me superbly. She has, as far as I can tell from the outside, a pair of tits no king ever had. I shall either marry her or murder her.

DEVIL (*stepping out, to himself*): An estimable man! (*Aloud*) Count Blockhead, if I'm not mistaken?

MURDRAX: Baron Murdrax, if you don't want a thrashing.

DEVIL: Your Lordship is infatuated with the young Baroness?

MURDRAX (*groaning*): Beyond all measure!

DEVIL: Then I shall procure her for you.

MURDRAX: How?

DEVIL: But only under certain conditions.

MURDRAX: Stipulate whatever you wish!

DEVIL: First, you must make your eldest son study philosophy.

MURDRAX: Good.

DEVIL: Secondly, you must murder thirteen apprentice tailors.

MURDRAX: Do you take me for a fool, you scoundrel? What kind of crazy conditions are these? To murder thirteen apprentice tailors! And why, of all people, apprentice tailors?

DEVIL: Because they're the most innocent.

MURDRAX: How true!—But thirteen! What a mob! No, if necessary I'll lop off seven heads, but not a single head more!

DEVIL *(insulted)*: What's this? Do you think you can bargain with me like a Jew? *(He starts to exit.)*

MURDRAX: Listen, my man, I'll do away with nine—eleven—yes, even twelve; only spare me the thirteenth—that would go beyond the even number limit!

DEVIL: Good, I'll settle for twelve, if you'll just break a couple of lousy ribs of Number Thirteen.

MURDRAX: Well, if it's just a couple of lousy ribs, I won't mind! But—but—

DEVIL: What? Another but?

MURDRAX: Yes, look here! I'm wearing a new coat and weskit, and they're bound to get all bloodied up in this mass slaughter!

DEVIL: Oh, if it's only that! You can simply tie a napkin over them.

MURDRAX: May the Devil take me, but that's it! I'll tie on a napkin!

DEVIL: And tomorrow I shall wait for you by the hunting lodge in the woods at Lopsbrunn. Once there you can take off the napkin and take up the Baroness in your arms!

MURDRAX: Ho ho ho! Naturally I won't need a napkin for that! *(Exits.)*

DEVIL: "Well, it worked!" as Octavio Piccolomini said to Max.[*] Judging by my ability to read faces, I'm not going to have any further trouble with Sir Wattsdale, because he looks exactly like the pious Aeneas whom I saw running away from Dido yesterday noon, three thousand years ago.

---

[*] From Schiller's *Wallensteins Tod*, Act II, Scene 5, last verse but one.

ACT TWO, SCENE 1

(Enter Wattsdale.)

WATTSDALE *(talking to himself)*: And soon the wedding will take place! My bride is clever, beautiful, and high-minded. But I'm twelve thousand Reichstaler in debt, and she's too shrewd to hand me over such a sum without further ado. I wish she were on Bald Mountain and I had her purse in my pocket!

DEVIL *(stepping out, to himself)*: Another estimable man! *(Aloud)* Your servant, Sir Wattsdale. How are things?

WATTSDALE: Miserable, Sir Bishop.

DEVIL: How much do you want for your bride?

WATTSDALE *(enraged)*: Sir, you—!

DEVIL: I am just a passionate collector of illegitimate June bugs, fat innkeepers, and young brides, and wouldn't haggle much over the price.

WATTSDALE: Ah! A collector! And wouldn't haggle!—What do you offer me then for Liddy? She's a capital beauty all right.

DEVIL: For her beauty, I offer two thousand Reichstaler in legal tender.

WATTSDALE: She has a brain.

DEVIL: For that I deduct five groschen, two pfennig. It's a shortcoming on a girl.

WATTSDALE: She has a fine, soft hand.

DEVIL: What makes for soft slaps on the ear. I'll pay you seven thousand Reichstaler in gold for that.

WATTSDALE: She is still chaste!

DEVIL *(making a sour face)*: Ah, chastity here, chastity there— I can't give you any more than three groschen, one pfennig in copper for that.

WATTSDALE: Sir, are you unaware that a pound of mutton costs more than four groschen in currency?

DEVIL: Pooh! Ever since the dimmer street lighting and the introduction of the border tariff, mutton has become very expensive and chastity extraordinarily cheap. In Berlin, for example, one can buy a portion of chastity in the evening for

two, three, or when it's high, four counterfeit silver groschen, not counting the discount.
WATTSDALE: But Liddy also has feeling, imagination—
DEVIL: Feeling ruins the complexion; imagination causes blue rings under the eyes and spoils the works. For the whole mess, I offer you, to put it ironically, thruppence.
WATTSDALE: Your taste is rather revolting.
DEVIL: In a word, if once and for all you shut your mouth about the possibly ethical qualities of the Baroness, which are not conducive to my well-being, I'll give you another eleven thousand Reichstaler in Dutch ring ducats. And now, I ask you, doesn't my bid seem acceptable?
WATTSDALE: How much does that amount to, altogether?
DEVIL (*counting on his fingers*): For her Beauty, two thousand Reichstaler in legal tender. For her Chastity, three groschen, one pfennig in copper. For her soft hand, seven thousand Reichstaler in gold. For her Feeling and Imagination, thruppence—to put it ironically. And for your shutting up about her ethical qualities, eleven thousand Reichstaler in Dutch ring ducats. Altogether that makes twenty thousand Reichstaler, three groschen, four pfennig. From that, however, I deduct five groschen, two pfennig for her brain—thus there remain 19,999 Reichstaler, twenty-two groschen, two pfennig.
WATTSDALE: Agreed, Mr. Bride-and-Junebug Collector!—When do I get the money?
DEVIL: At once!—But promise this first: to lure Liddy into the hunting lodge at Lopsbrunn tomorrow morning, to prevent the servants from accompanying her, and not to track down afterward the person who shall abduct her from there.
WATTSDALE: I can guarantee all that—except for the condition that I lure the Baroness to Lopsbrunn, for that would be thought suspicious. I advise you to let esthetic Ratbane suggest to Liddy a drive out there. He reads a great deal in the writings of the new Romantic School and is giddy over cottages in the woods.

DEVIL: I'll try to persuade him to do so. For this restriction, however, you must be satisfied if I settle half the account in Austrian paper currency.

WATTSDALE: Why, dammit Sir, but you're stingy!

DEVIL *(feeling flattered, smirks)*: Oh, I beg you—why, you make me blush! Indeed, I like to be damned, like to be called stingy, in fact love it, but I'm still far from being stingy enough! *(Exits with Wattsdale.)*

SCENE 2

Ratbane's Room

RATBANE *(seated at a table, trying to write a poem)*: Ah, ideas! Plenty of rhymes, but ideas! Ideas! Here I sit, drink coffee, chew pencils, write down this, cross out that, and can't find one idea, not a single idea!—Ha, now what should I make of that?—Wait a minute! Was that an idea which just struck me?—Magnificent! Divine! I shall compose a sonnet precisely on the idea that I can't find any ideas. Indeed, this idea about the absolute loss of ideas is the most brilliant idea that could ever have occurred to me! I'll write a poem about the very fact, as it were, that I'm unable to write a poem at all! How piquant! How original! *(He runs quickly to the mirror.)* Upon my word, I do look quite like a genius! *(He sits down at the table.)* Now I shall begin! *(He writes, speaking lines aloud)*

Sonnet

I sat down at my table chewing quills,
Just like——

Hm, what in the world so sits that it looks like me when I chew a quill? Where can I find an appropriate image for that? I'll run to the window and see if I can't observe something similar outside! *(He opens the window and looks out.)* There's a boy sitting and shitting—No, it doesn't look like that! But across the way, there's a toothless old beggar sitting on that stone bench biting a piece of hard bread—no, that would be too trivial, too commonplace! *(He closes the window again and paces up and down the room.)* Hm, hm! No inspiration? Then I shall enumerate everything that chews. A cat chews, a polecat chews, a lion—stop! A lion!—What does a lion chew? He chews either a sheep, or an ox, or a goat, or a horse —stop! A horse!—Now, what the mane is to a horse, the quill is to a pen. Thus both look somewhat alike—*(Shouting)* Eureka, there's the image! Bold, daring, new, Calderonian!

I was sitting at my table chewing quills,
Just like
(While he writes it down)
the lion, 'ere the gray of dawn
The horse's rapid-running quill does chew on—

(He reads the last two lines over again, aloud, and smacks his lips as though they tasted good.) No, no! Never before has there been such a metaphor! I shudder before my own poetic powers! *(Cosily slurping down a cup of coffee)* A horse, a lion's quill! And then that epithet "rapid-running"! How apt! How apropos! For what quill could run more rapidly than a horse? Also, the phrase "'ere the gray of dawn"—that's genuinely Homeric! Of course, they make absolutely no sense here, but they do complete the picture. They make for an epic in miniature! Oh, I must run to the mirror again! *(Contemplating himself therein)* By Jove, a most brilliant face! True, the nose is somewhat colossal, but that's how it is! *Ex ungue leonem* *—for by his nose, you know a genius!

(Enter the Devil.)

DEVIL: *Bon jour*, Mr. Ratbane!
RATBANE *(turns around and, just as he is about to greet the*

---

* "By the claw [you know] the lion."

ACT TWO, SCENE 2

Devil, he notices the horse-hoof from which the wrappings have slipped down): God almighty, the Devil! *(He tries to rush past the Devil and gain the door.)*

DEVIL *(sees his bare hoof and stamps furiously, pawing the ground with it)*: Abominable carelessness! *(To Ratbane)* Don't be alarmed! I've read your poems!

RATBANE *(immediately cajoled)*: You have? You have?

DEVIL: Yes, and they pleased me exceedingly.

RATBANE *(completely entrusting)*: Oh, you bestow upon me praise which I can hardly—you write poetry too?

DEVIL: I—

RATBANE *(not letting a word out of his mouth)*: You must write poetry! Do try it! I'm sure you will compose magnificent poems!

DEVIL *(aside)*: Because I praised his.

RATBANE: I only beg you to write under another name. Not because you need be ashamed of your poetry, as is the fashion, but rather to conceal that which is characteristic of your name. Just as a person, for example, who's very twisted and gloomy could be called *bright*,* so you could call yourself Angel, Heaven, or Virtue.

DEVIL: You give advice worth following, Mr. Ratbane! After all, I have already brought forth several works, such as, only recently, "The French Revolution, a Tragedy in Fourteen Years, with a Prologue by Louis XV." † The play has been very badly received, however, largely by virtue of its fatal error: it guillotined the critics. Besides, I can't get to play a second run either in Prussia, Austria, or England, in spite of many friends working underground on it there. The censorship is too rigid. Still, I have hopes that it will be revived

---

* A play on words impossible to duplicate in English. The original has "hell" (bright, clear), which is at the same time a pun on Theodor *Hell*, one of the authors satirized in Act I, Scene 3.
† Other editions add here: "and a Chorus of Emigrés."

again in Spain with a few minor changes.* I am working now on a farce to be published by the Sultan of Turkey's press, under the title "The Greek War for Freedom by the Author of the French Revolution."

RATBANE: I see I've been acquainted with your writings for some time now, Mr. Devil, without knowing you as their author. And they do have something undeniably colossal about them! But the incredible liberties you take with time and place—they're just too much! And even worse, the *verse!* The *verse!* Also, the views of the world expressed in them might—

DEVIL: And do you happen to know what the world is?

RATBANE: What a question! The world is the essence of all existence, from the smallest worm to the most immense solar system.

DEVIL: So let me tell you, then, that this essence of the All, which you honor with the name "world," is nothing more than a mediocre, indifferent comedy. It has been smeared together during vacations by a beardless, loud-mouthed angel, who, if I'm not mistaken, is still in the twelfth grade and lives in the ordinary world that is incomprehensible to man. The copy in which we are found is on the shelves of the lending library at X, I believe. It is being read at this very moment by a beautiful lady known to the author. She intends to hand him her opinion of it at teatime this evening—that is to say, over six trillion years from now.

RATBANE: Sir, I'm going mad! If the world is a comedy, what then is Hell, which is also in the world?

DEVIL: Hell is the ironical part of the play, and, as usually happens, the twelfth-grader did better by it than by Heaven, which should be the pure, serene part of the world.

---

* Other editions add: "provided the Duke of Angoulême doesn't drink up all my Spanish bitters." Louis Antoine de Bourbon, Duke of Angoulême (1775–1844), was the eldest son of Count Artois, later King Charles X. An ardent defender of royalist ideas, in 1823 he suppressed the Spanish Revolution.

ACT TWO, SCENE 2   33

RATBANE: And could Hell really be nothing more than that?—How—then how are criminals punished?

DEVIL: We keep laughing at a murderer until finally he laughs at himself for having taken the trouble to kill someone. The severest punishment for one of the damned, however, is simply this: he must read the *Evening News* * and the *Freethinker*,† but is not allowed to spit on them.

RATBANE: Lord in Heaven, Mr. Devil, I note that not only my poetry, but all world literature as well, is known in Hell. How is that to be explained?

DEVIL: Quite naturally! Not only the Bad comes to Hell, but also the Wretched, the Deplorable, and the Trivial. Thus even the good Cicero sits there as well as the nasty Catiline. Since nowadays the more recent German literature is the most miserable of the Miserable, for preference we occupy ourselves with that.

RATBANE: Why, if German literature is the chief business in Hell, what kind of curious sidelines might you practice down there?

DEVIL: Well, during off-hours we usually make windowpanes or eyeglass lenses out of ghosts, because they are invisible and for that reason also transparent. Thus recently, when my grandmother had a strange whim to look into the essence of Virtue, she set the philosophers Kant and Aristotle upon her nose, but, as she looked through them it became steadily darker, and so she made herself a lorgnette out of two Pomeranian farmers instead. She then saw as clearly as ever she could have wished.

RATBANE (*clapping his hands together over his head*): Amazing! Amazing! Tell me, do you know your way about Heaven too?

---

* *Die Abendzeitung*, published in Dresden during 1817–1821 under the joint editorship of Theodor Hell and Friedrich Kind; and from 1822–1843 under Hell alone. See previous note on Hell.

† *Der Freimütige* (1803–1834). During the period 1808–1829, edited by August von Kotzebue and August Kuhn with the subtitle, "*Unterhaltungsblatt für gebildete unbefangene Leser.*" See note on Kuhn.

DEVIL: Why not? Only the other day Zamiel from *Der Freischütz** came down to Hell. He pretended to be a cousin of mine, but because of the generosity he had shown his hunting boy Max, I had to use force in leading him back to Heaven. True, he resisted terribly, but finally, after I punched an iron ring through his nose, he said in a hollow voice, "Time will tell," and followed me to the gates of Heaven, where Socrates received him with open arms and led him at once to the barber to have his beard sheared off and look a little more civilized.

RATBANE: Oh, since you are so well acquainted up in Heaven, I entreat you, do tell me what they are doing, those immortal heroes of virtue, those whom I have chosen as the guiding stars of my life and poetry! Above all, what deeds is he performing, that sublime paragon of friendship, the divine Marquis of Posa?

DEVIL: You mean the one in *Don Carlos*?

RATBANE: The same, the Knight of Malta!

DEVIL: If you think he's in Heaven, you're mistaken—he sits with me in Hell.

RATBANE: What?

DEVIL: Yes, yes. The Marquis of Posa, finding himself all of a sudden in Hell, was just as surprised as Zamiel finding himself in Heaven. But we took away his resounding speaking trumpet and made him take up the vocation for which he was most talented. He has become a panderer and set up an alehouse which he calls "At the Queen Elizabeth de Valois."

RATBANE: Impossible! Impossible! Posa an innkeeper? I can't imagine it!

DEVIL: Don't fret! His present position seems to suit him well. He's getting fat and already has a paunch.

---

* Karl Maria von Weber's opera *Der Freischütz*, which opened in Berlin on June 18, 1821, with libretto by Friedrich Kind, member of the pseudo-romantic Dresden "Liederkreis."

ACT TWO, SCENE 2

RATBANE: A paunch?—But what about that other famous model of self-sacrifice, the noble, magnificent painter, Spinarosa? * Surely he sits in the front ranks of the blessed, right next to Curtius and Regulus?

DEVIL: No, you're off in your calculations again! Spinarosa is employed in Posa's tavern as headwaiter. There he practices that self-denial which, heretofore, much as he wished, he could never quite come around to. But now, when he has to serve a guest a tankard of Merseburger, his eager, drooling mouth shows only too clearly that sacrificing this mug costs him much more in self-control than did giving up the tedious, dull Camilla. Recently he even tried to steal a sip on the sly, but Posa dealt him such a clout behind the ears it took him two weeks to forget it.

RATBANE: God! How could anyone be so mistaken! Posa deals Spinarosa a clout on the ear! I'm speechless!—And you call Camilla tedious! No, you can't be serious, Your Devilish Majesty! Oh, I beg you, how does she fare, this ideal creature of love? This woman who, even in the later, so-called best years of her life, even after bearing him a son who has passed his sixteenth birthday, nonetheless never once forgot her beloved, and indeed still sighs sweetly after him, as if she were only eighteen. Oh, surely she, the sublime one, together with Thekla and Julia, now glides over the fields of eternal peace!

DEVIL: Yes, she did reach Heaven, and attached herself to the two girls. When, however, Thekla once absent-mindedly called her "Mother," it made her so furious she came down to us in Hell. Here she stood all alone for three weeks, resuming without interruption the contemplations she had begun in Heaven as to whether or not she could really see. Finally Falstaff, by chance, passed by, thirsting strongly again for champagne and other sweets, and I don't know yet just how it happened, but he mistook Camilla for a glass of syrup,

---

* Spinarosa, and Camilla, the daughter of the Duchess of Sorrento, are important characters in Houwald's tragedy, *Das Bild*. See note, p. 18.

picked her up in his hand, and swilled her right down. Afterward he complained to me that the syrup must have been very bad, because it had given him a terrible belly-ache.

RATBANE: I despair, and almost lack the courage to question any further. How then are my favorite tragic heroes, Schiller's Wallenstein and Müllner's Hugo? *

DEVIL: They're both in Hell. When he was dying, Hugo thought Heaven would open up for him, but, as is easily possible with any dying person, he was mistaken. Naturally his brother snatched the revenging sword away from the cherub, though not to throw it away, but rather personally to behead his murderer. And if in so doing he winked and smiled, he acted as one does with a young, unruly dog, coaxing him on with gesture and grimace, only to thrash him that much more soundly afterward.—Now, as for Wallenstein, we found out after thorough examination that he was excellently qualified to be the principal of a school. So we immediately installed him in our Infernal Academy at Z, and would have found him most satisfactory but for one shortcoming: every time he lifted his stick to discipline a worthless brat, he'd keep on yelling "There isn't room here to hit him," "Well, here goes anyway," "I'd still rather not do it," and so on, for so long that by the time he finished, the brat had stuck a large paper pigtail on him from behind.

RATBANE: May the Devil—(*Correcting himself with a bow*) May Mr. Devil whisk me off, if my breath be not taken away with astonishment and wonder! Still, carry on! What are the poets themselves doing? Schiller, Shakespeare, Calderon, Dante, Ariosto, Horace? How do they keep busy? What are they working at?

DEVIL: Shakespeare is writing commentaries on Franz Horn; †

---

* Hugo, Count Orindur, hero of Müllner's tragedy *Guilt* (*Die Schuld*).
† Franz Horn (1781–1837), writer and literary historian, lectured on Shakespeare in Berlin during Grabbe's sojourn there.

ACT TWO, SCENE 2

Dante has just thrown Ernst Schulze * out the window; Horace has married Maria Stuart; Schiller sighs over Baron Auffenberg; † Ariosto bought a new umbrella; Calderon reads your poetry, heartily requests to be remembered to you, and advises you to visit the hunting lodge in the woods near Lopsbrunn in the company of Liddy, because this little cottage lies in a truly romantic region.

RATBANE: O fortunate me! O most fortunate man that I am! I'll climb to the top of the roof for joy! Calderon reads my poetry! Calderon sends me his greetings! I could consume a candle with joy! Greet the Señor de la Barca a thousand times more, tell him that I am his most passionate admirer, that I will go to the hunting lodge with Liddy even if I have to break off her legs, that I—

DEVIL: Enough! My time is up!—If you should ever need me, you know, of course, where I live—in Hell. It's a bit far from the village, but if you want to get there in a hurry, you must travel by way of Berlin, where you go to the King's Wall, or by Dresden, where you look up Fish Alley, or Leipzig, where it's Prussian Row, or through Paris via the Palais Royal. Tartarus is but five minutes away from any of these places, and you will find only the best well-maintained roads from there on. Indeed, it will soon be dark! Sleep only so so! *(He starts to exit.)*

RATBANE *(stopping him)*: By the way! Just one last word! May I not be let in on why you have come up to visit Earth?

DEVIL: Because they're housecleaning down in Hell!

RATBANE: I thank you for your most obliging answer. Have a good sleep.

DEVIL: Sleep only so so! *(Exits.)*

---

* Ernst Schulze (1789–1817), author of the romantic tale in verse, "The Enchanted Rose" ("Die bezauberte Rose"), lectured as Privatdozent in Göttingen on ancient languages and literatures.
† Joseph, Freiherr von Auffenberg (1798–1857), was associated with the theater in Karlsruhe. Later in life he wrote a number of historical dramas, largely in imitation of Schiller.

SCENE 3

A Height on the Outskirts of the Village

(Enter Mushcliff.)

MUSHCLIFF: See, there it lies, my home town! Hark, the vesper bell in the gray church steeple is ringing! How pleasant it sounds after three years absence! Even the ancient castle has remained unchanged. Proud and stately it rises there out of the midst of its blooming summer garden, and the first glimmer of the sunset glow makes purple plays of light on its mighty casement windows! . . . O Liddy! O Liddy! How I do love thee! *(Vexed)* If only I weren't so damned ugly!

(Enter the Schoolmaster.)

SCHOOLMASTER *(not noticing Mushcliff)*: Here will I take my stand, look down upon the plains of my schoolship, and indulge my patriotic reveries. How much everything could be improved! If the farmers were forced to attend school until they learned something, even after Doomsday they'd still have to be kept there with only bread and water for a full six weeks. Moreover, what sort of practical application might be made of that large oak forest over there? Ah, when will the happy day of the Enlightenment dawn, the day when the trees will be cut into schoolbenches, these benches systematically arranged and set up in the fields, knowledge-hungry boys and young men drawn to them, and me created director of it all? Oh, then, with the help of a balloon, I would make the evening sun my glowing lectern, I would use the church steeple as a pen, that lake would be my inkwell, and that mountain would be a side of bacon which parents and patrons

out of gratitude would give me. *(He sinks into profound meditation.)*
MUSHCLIFF *(steps forward and slaps him on the shoulder)*: There you are, lost in genuine pedagogical revery, Professor!
SCHOOLMASTER *(looking up at him)*: Mr. Mushcliff?!—I'm delighted—what a pleasant surprise! . . . How did you like Italy, the land where the stones speak? Any signs of old age yet on the Venus de Medici? I hope the Pope's boots hadn't trod the dung before you kissed his foot? Is—
MUSHCLIFF: I'll relate it all at a more convenient time. Only tell me, is everything here the same as before?
SCHOOLMASTER: Nothing out of the ordinary has occurred during your absence. Yesterday the fire engine was repaired to prevent day-before-yesterday's fire. And rich Bartholomew married Katherine with whom he was so yearningly in love. He has now had a shirt made out of the same buckskin as his trousers because his wife's fisticuffs pained him so. As far as my own humble self is concerned, it's been with me as with old father Homer—I haven't tasted roast pork in two years.
MUSHCLIFF: Why, what brings you to the conclusion that old Homer never tasted roast pork?
SCHOOLMASTER: Because he *described* it with such discernment, Mr. Mushcliff.
MUSHCLIFF: Then it follows that you must describe brandy very badly?
SCHOOLMASTER: No, not brandy—virtue.
MUSHCLIFF: Still, there's no rule without an exception!——But tell me, how are things up at the castle? Is Miss Liddy still bright and gay?
SCHOOLMASTER: A chimney sweep has come to the castle. He calls himself a bishop and seems to have made reservations for the loss of his innocence two weeks before his birth.— The cheerfulness of the Baroness and her uncle's bad temper rest at *status quo.*

MUSHCLIFF: There! For your good tidings, twenty condoms! *
I bought them off a Jew, as that was the only way I could
break loose from him, and I've no further use for them.
(Exits.)
SCHOOLMASTER: Condoms? What kind of things are these?
What should I, a haggard schoolmaster, do with them?—
But wait! I shall send them over to the magistrate's wife in
exchange for a pot of peas she gave me. She's an expert on
everything, and will know best how to place the condoms.

(Enter Tobias.)

TOBIAS: Good evening, Mr. Schoolmaster.
SCHOOLMASTER: Good evening, Tobias! *(Aside)* How the devil
can I shake this fellow off?
TOBIAS: Well now, how's my little Gottlieb doing? Have you
taken him up to the castle?
SCHOOLMASTER: Haven't you also heard, Mr. Tobias, that a
dentist who pulls teeth for nothing arrived at the inn an
hour ago?
TOBIAS: It's all the same to me! See, I've got two good rows of
teeth so strong and healthy I can whet my pitchfork on them.
SCHOOLMASTER: What does that matter? Now you can get them
pulled out for nothing! You can't miss a bargain like that!
TOBIAS: Yes, that's true enough! You can't pass up a little profit!
I'll go and let him rip out all of my back molars! *(Exits.)*
SCHOOLMASTER: O holy simplicity! Sweet innocence! Thou hast
abandoned the Luxury of the Cities and taken refuge in the
Hovel of the Peasant! Tobias lets his teeth be pulled because
he can get it done for nothing. Oh! Oh! Oh! *(Exits.)*

---

* Condoms: already in use during the 18th century. Thought by some to be named after Dr. Condom, or Conton, 18th-century English physician, supposedly their inventor. Upon Kettembeil's censorship of this passage, Grabbe substituted: "a copy of the 'Memoirs of Jacob Casanova de Seingalt' bound in morocco, but, for all that, hidebound."

SCENE 4

A Room in the Castle

(Enter Liddy and the Baron.)

BARON: Let this be a warning, my child! I do not trust Sir Wattsdale at all!
LIDDY: He has his shortcomings, but that he possesses some manly qualities too, was demonstrated only recently in his duel with Count Naubek.
BARON: In his duel? Oh, yes. Two young gentlemen did fight a duel yesterday. It seems that one of them swore upon his honor that he had already stood at the whipping post a number of times, while the other simply refused to believe him!—Good night! I've said enough! *(Exits.)*
LIDDY: As a matter of fact, Uncle's warnings are beginning to take effect! Wattsdale is not the man I took him for when we first met! . . . Strange that against my will a certain Mushcliff strikes my fancy—he had the ugliest face imaginable, yet he was the most gifted and excellent man I've ever known.

(Enter a servant.)

SERVANT: A Mr. Mushcliff is waiting in the hall.
LIDDY *(astonished)*: Who?—Mushcliff?—What does he look like?
SERVANT: We just pulled seven old women out of the castle pond. They threw themselves terror-stricken into it at the sight of his face.
LIDDY *(to herself)*: Beyond a doubt, it is he! *(Aloud)* Show him in! *(Exit servant.)* It will cost me some pains to hide my astonishment.

42 JEST, SATIRE, IRONY

(Enter Mushcliff.)

MUSHCLIFF: Ha, there I perceive her once again! *(Aloud)* Madam, I have just returned from Italy and hasten to greet you.

LIDDY: Welcome home, Mr. Mushcliff, welcome home!—Did Italy live up to your expectations? How did you like Rome?

MUSHCLIFF: Gray ruins peep out from green shrubbery, loud footsteps resound down lonely streets, and whoever gazes upon this seven-hilled city of the past from the ruins of the Capitol, and hears the last rumblings of a passing storm dying out over the distant horizon, feels quite differently moved than he would were his lookout a churchtower in Berlin!

LIDDY: It seems to me that in Rome Death might not be too painful.

MUSHCLIFF: But certainly! Indeed, there one is almost ashamed to be alive!

LIDDY: Did you look up my brother in Florence?

MUSHCLIFF: Here are letters from him and his wife!

LIDDY: Oh, hurry! *(She opens the letters.)*

MUSHCLIFF *(observing her while she reads)*: What a charming woman! One can hear the music of her movements! The unquenchable flames of her eyes sparkle like two volatile naptha-fires, and her bosom swells gently over her heart like a lake over its well-springs! Happy the chosen one who can rest his weary head upon such bliss! *(Pacing up and down)* No, I'll be damned if I can stand this any longer! I must find out if there's any hope for me, or whether I should hang myself from that oak tree! Ugly or not ugly, I am going to declare my love to her now, do or die! *(He steps up to Liddy.)* Miss Liddy, do not let my proposal frighten you, for I myself know only too well that my waist is enough to make horses shy away, mistaking it as they do for an abandoned road crossing—that my boots, even with my calves tucked inside them, are as empty as a pair of hollowed-out tree trunks—that my ears—

ACT TWO, SCENE 4

LIDDY: For heaven's sake, Mr. Mushcliff, are you delirious?

MUSHCLIFF: And my nose! Ho ho, my nose! All mankind shudders at the sight of it! As misshapen as a tiger's intestines, as red as a fox, as flat as a story by Karoline Pichler,* and as brief as a second.

LIDDY: As a second!—How long is your right arm?

MUSHCLIFF: As long as a leap year! Standing at attention I can button my shoes with it! When I say "standing at attention," however, I don't mean to compare myself with a Prussian guardsman, but rather with a Leipzig militiaman. Only the hangman knows where my back learned its excessive servility. I am bent in a permanent bow, tirelessly observing my own legs, which look not unlike two corpulent Turkish scimitars!

LIDDY: Leave those corpulent scimitars out of the picture, and relieve at last my amazement and curiosity! What is this enthusiastic self-portrayal of yours supposed to lead up to?

MUSHCLIFF: To this: that I throw myself at your feet, that I worship you, that I love you!

LIDDY: Well, I must grant you this: you do know how to lead up to a declaration of love! Though you start off with descriptions of your person from which I should sooner have surmised that, with those legs, you were going to become a baker, than that you were ready to declare your love for me.

MUSHCLIFF: Oh, do not break my heart over my legs! No man can hate these two antipodes of horror, these two wreckers of friendship, these two cure-alls of love, more fiercely than I! Say I were to save the life of some nobleman who had fallen into a swamp, and were then to press him to my breast in eternal union of our two souls, he'd strike me and run away, should he even so much as glance at my legs! But for all that, Madam, the power of passion makes me stammer out anew my pledge of love! It has reached such a point that I am now

---

* Karoline Pichler (1769–1843), a minor Austrian writer of historical novels, stories, and some dramas.

ashamed to eat beef with mustard, as they seem too common for a lover—and that, in my ecstasy, I've written an insipid tragedy too foolish in content for me not to relate it to you immediately. Instead of Fate, I let my tragedy be governed by *Ennui*, the goddess of the Anti-Fatalists. At the start of the scene with the despondent people, this divinity is honored by a reading from the dramatic works of Eduard Gehe.* Unexpectedly, a declaration resounds from within the temple that the goddess has decreed the downfall of the exalted Princess Salvavenia.† The people howl, the bells ring out, the Princess wails as if she were already in Satan's clutches, and everybody rushes off the stage in wild confusion. At this very moment, Ossian enters eating bread and butter. When he has finished, the scene changes to the audience-chamber of the Kaiser's palace. The Kaiser is wearing a Napoleonic waistcoat, while the lords and nobles are standing around His Majesty, dressed in gray leggings they have unbuttoned for grief. In one corner of the room, there are two stockings, wrangling bitterly, each wanting to poison the other. A plush jerkin hangs nearby, turning the pages of an encyclopedia and drinking a cup of tea. Whereupon a revenge-seeking hypochondriacal broomstick with bloodthirsty mien slinks in and—

LIDDY: Good gracious, stop! I fear I shall lose my reason!

MUSHCLIFF: I only wanted to show you to what mad compositions the power of love has driven me! ‡

LIDDY: I hope you're not quite so serious about this love of yours, for I am engaged to Sir Wattsdale.

MUSHCLIFF: Alas, then let the earth swallow me! Unhappy wretch that I am!—Engaged?—Indeed, my tears roll down!

---

* Eduard Heinrich Gehe (1793–1845), author of a number of Schillerlike historical dramas (*Gustav Adolf, Dido, Anna Boleyn*), various opera libretti, and novellas. Part of the Dresden "Liederkreis."
† From the Latin, *salva venia*: "with permission to say."
‡ In other editions, Mushcliff replies: "I only wanted to show you that love has already robbed me of mine."

(Passing his hand over his forehead) If—if in this my sorrow I should do away with myself, then I shall have to shoot myself. For were I to drown myself, I would have to worry about getting the sniffles—and to stand before God's Judgment Seat sneezing would not only be rather disquieting, but most unseemly. *(Exits.)*

LIDDY: That man could please a girl more than he thinks.

ACT THREE

SCENE 1

Evening. Schoolmaster's room, in lamplight.

Schoolmaster and Blacksmith are in conversation.

BLACKSMITH: Yes, Mr. Schoolmaster, he had a cloven hoof and a tufted heel!

SCHOOLMASTER: It's the Devil, Konrad, it's the Devil! Any textbook of natural history will tell you the Devil has a horse's hoof!

BLACKSMITH: And he yelled after me that he was Satan, and threatened to wring my neck if I spread the news.

SCHOOLMASTER: Ho ho, don't worry about that! I have other plans for him!—What do you say we catch Old Harry, lock him in a cage, then make the rounds of the markets and fairs, setting him up as a *Mermaid*, or, to make the posters even more attractive, as a *Mer-ry Widow*, and bill ourselves as two professors of mermaidry?

BLACKSMITH: We'd grow very rich!

SCHOOLMASTER: Or we could even present him to the public exactly as he is—the Devil. Then we'd make him dance, letting him jump to the tune "How lovely lights our way the morning star!" and put our heads down his throat every fifteen minutes as if he were a trained lion, all to the amazement of the onlookers.

BLACKSMITH: This head-putting-down-the-throat business might be very difficult—he has a rather small snout.

SCHOOLMASTER (*walking up and down the room in proud, stately*

46

ACT THREE, SCENE 1

strides): You pitiful, doubting Thomas! I've rammed far more difficult things than that into the heads of my pupils.

BLACKSMITH: I haven't seen any sign of it yet in my boy Georgie.

SCHOOLMASTER: Your Georgie! That stupid sack of potatoes! The wise Confucius himself, though he never saw hops or malt, would have lost several wagonloads on him—Confidentially, what was your wife thinking about when pregnant with him? The boy's got a head like a horse.

BLACKSMITH: Oh, that's all due to that cursed stallion that tore himself loose during a shoeing, and stared through the window right into my wife's face as she stood in the parlor pouring vinegar onto the salad.

(Enter Gretchen.)

GRETCHEN: Good evening, Schoolmaster! The magistrate's wife ordered me to call you an impertinent ox and to throw these condoms in your face!

SCHOOLMASTER *(while picking up the condoms)*: Hm, hm! Has Madam no use for these things, then, in her housekeeping?

GRETCHEN: Ah, the Professor, how ignorant he is! Such goods were not designed for housekeeping, as any Christian soul could tell a mile away. Madam is beside herself with rage.

SCHOOLMASTER: Hm! hm! But there are only sixteen here, and I sent Madam twenty—what's happened to the other four?

GRETCHEN: Well, in the height of her scolding, Madam stuck the best four into her knitting bag.

SCHOOLMASTER: In the height of her scolding, into her knitting bag? Uhum! What puzzling inconsistency!

GRETCHEN: Adieu, Schoolmaster! *(Exits.)*

SCHOOLMASTER: Smithy, Smithy, now I've got it! This is how we're going to lure the Devil into our hands! Can you build a bird cage?

BLACKSMITH: I think so, yes.

SCHOOLMASTER: Well then, run—run and make me one tonight as big as a man, with a door six-feet high. And tomorrow evening I shall place it in the woods, lay the condoms inside, and hide in the bushes. Now, with a fellow like the Devil, one can always presume he goes out stealing wood. When, while making his rounds, he nears the cage, I hope the condoms—which, according to the Magistrate's wife who stuck four of them into her knitting bag, must be especially sinful—will lure him irresistibly, due to the magnetic power with which Satan is drawn to Evil, into the cage. Then I shall rush out, shut the door behind him, and whistle through my fingers.

BLACKSMITH *(trying to make the Schoolmaster an obliging compliment)*: Why, Schoolmaster, you puzzled that out downright philo–filou–sof—yeah, like a whale!

SCHOOLMASTER *(giving him a friendly pat on the shoulder)*: Philosophical is the word, my friend, philosophical! Etymologists trace it back to the phrase "Phil is so fickle." One has only to elide the words, change the vowel "i" in "is" to "o," drop the extra "s," which is, after all, a mere orthographical adjustment, substitute "p, h" for the "f" in fickle, making for more consistent spelling anyway, since Phil is spelled with "p, h," and, instead of that awkward "k, l, e" ending, simplify it all to "al"—and the word "philosophical" is most unphilosophically, but philologically correctly explained and deduced.*

BLACKSMITH *(as if he has understood him)*: Quite right, Mr. Schoolmaster! Deduced! That's the hitch, there's the rub!—Now "reduced" † is something else again. Oh, oh, we smithies aren't so dumb, we smithies aren't so dumb! *(Exits.)*

---

* Here the translator has had to take the liberty of trying to do in English what Grabbe did in German but, of necessity, with entirely different words. The original is a play on the similarity in sound, in German, of *philosophisch* (philosophic) and *viele Strohwisch* (many wisps of straw).

† Here again, the word "reduced" does not translate the German *officer*—nor does it make any more sense than the original. Apparently Grabbe used *officer* because to the blacksmith's raw ears *Deduziert* sounded like *Offizier*; and so, in English, I have him hear the (to him) unusual word "deduced" as "reduced."

ACT THREE, SCENE 1

SCHOOLMASTER *(while getting into a dressing gown)*: My, it's late already—I'll just pour myself a small glass of stomach tonic and then jump into bed.—What! Who's knocking so late? Come in!

(Enter Ratbane and Mushcliff.)

RATBANE: Sorry to disturb you like this at bedtime, Schoolmaster! But do you have any prescription against shooting oneself? Mr. Mushcliff is coming down with the disease.

SCHOOLMASTER: If I might suggest anything, how about some quack medicine—say, a dose of eight to twelve bottles of wine? They might at least defer the damage a little.

RATBANE: *Bene*, Schoolmaster! A dozen bottles of wine! Presto! Close the shutters! We're going to make a jolly night of it! What do you say, Mushcliff?

MUSHCLIFF: All right then. In the name of Hell, let it be! Pain is the foil of joy, and so I will use my pain for it! Here's the gold! Produce the wine, Schoolmaster. If, after all this, I'm still determined to shoot myself, there'll be plenty of time to make up for it tomorrow.

SCHOOLMASTER *(who has plunged into the liveliest activity)*: Hurrah! Tweedledum and Tweedledee! That was spoken like a man, Mr. Mushcliff, and "Let There Be Wine" is my motto! *(He rushes over to the bedroom door.)* Little Gottlieb, little Gottlieb! Get up! Get up! Put on the lantern and light up your pants! Get up! Get up! You must come along to the tavern and help me tote back the wine.

(Little Gottlieb emerges from the bedroom half-asleep, his eyes blinking, wearing only a long nightshirt.)

LITTLE GOTTLIEB *(whining crankily)*: Ugh—hrmph—ugh! The room's steaming! The Turks are drumming!

SCHOOLMASTER: You rascal, are you crazy? What's got into you? There! Rub some water over your eyes! Quick! Quick! Quick! Where are your pants? Your jacket? Here, put on my coat! There! It fits you royally! Like a black velvet train! Now you look like a stage queen! Come, come, come on! (*Exits with Little Gottlieb.*)

MUSHCLIFF: Ha! Ha! Mr. Ratbane, you could easily insert that scene, without the least hesitation, into one of your own comedies.

RATBANE: O my God, Mushcliff, are you in your right mind? Such coarse, low comedy! Nowadays humor must be subtle, so subtle it can no longer be perceived. Then, should the audience nevertheless grasp it, it will be overjoyed—not, to be sure, with the play, but with its own cleverness at having found something where nothing was to be found. Moreover, the German is much too cultured and rational to tolerate strong, bold, genuine joviality.

MUSHCLIFF: Yes, yes. He does not laugh until he is sure that he will be able to account to himself afterward why he laughed.

RATBANE: Believe me, if anyone were really to write a comedy which, even down to its most unimportant detail, was based upon a profounder view of life, and dared carry out his ideas freely and originally, he would, for that very reason, be rejected by the vast majority of the public, who cannot see the forest for the trees.

MUSHCLIFF: It sounds as though you must have written such a comedy—and that it was a failure.

RATBANE: Ah, don't say "failure"! It sounds so cruel! "It wasn't a success," sounds much kinder.

MUSHCLIFF: May I make a suggestion? From now on, write nothing but tragedies. If you lend them the requisite mediocrity, they cannot fail to earn the most thundering applause. The plot, in particular, you must so fashion as to be charmingly flat and trivial—otherwise not every near-sighted sheepshead would be able to take it in. You must not expect the smallest understanding or spirit of inquiry from the reader. And if, by accident, a striking scene should creep in, be sure at the end to make a note of its significance and how it is to be related to the whole.—And you must of course knead everything sufficiently softly, for softness is pleasing even if it's but oozing mud.—But above all, always bear in mind the taste of the ladies, for they, though never recognized by a true poet as qualified judges, are now considered the highest court of appeal in the realm of art—whether they were so elected because of their nervous disorders or their skill in shredding lint is still an open question. All the more certain, however, is the fact that if, Mr. Ratbane, you have strength enough to scorn these rules, you will be decried as a blind, crazy, raw fantasist who wildly slops together beauties and paltriness. If, only now, Homer or Shakespeare were to publish their works for the first time, the reviews following might be expected to call the *Iliad* a senseless hodgepodge and *Lear* a bombastic pigsty. Yes, some critics might perhaps drop Homer a well-meaning hint that he model himself after *The Enchanted Rose*,* or order Shakespeare to study diligently the novels of Helmina von Chézy † and Fanny Tarnow ‡ that he may learn human psychology from them.

RATBANE *(who has coughed several times during Mushcliff's speech and shown signs of disapproval)*: My principles do not permit me to second your satirical attacks upon the rules. Rule seems to me rather indispensable. It is, so to speak, the trouserleg of genius. What else can the artist rely on, how can he come to an understanding, if not by virtue of his relationship to the critics, he—

MUSHCLIFF: The artist should be guided by his own genius. He should have a calm, clear understanding of the workings of his own mind. And, as for his relationship to the critics, let it be the following: the critics laboriously put up the

---

* *Die bezauberte Rose* (1818), a romantic tale in three cantos by Ernst Schulze. See previous note on Schulze.

† Helmina von Chézy (1783–1850), resident of Dresden and Vienna, was a dilettante author of the romantic school. She wrote *Lieder, Novellen,* opera libretti, and is best known for her libretto to Schubert's "Rosamunde."

‡ Fanny Tarnow (1779–1862), of Dresden, wrote fashionable novels, translated Balzac, George Sand, and, together with von Chézy, published the women's magazine *Iduna*.

barriers, making them only as wide as their brains, hence very narrow. Genius enters, finds them intolerably confining, knocks them down, and throws the pieces at the heads of the carping critics, making them howl in wild pandemonium. When the common rabble hears this outcry, it says in all its simplicity of soul, "They are criticizing"!

RATBANE: Hm, according to this, every badly reviewed poet will think you're on his side.

MUSHCLIFF: I am so far from being on his side that I have already censured the Government for its cruelty to the public in still hesitating to execute, once and for all, dozens of poets for their wretched poetry.

RATBANE (*in uncomprehending agitation*): No! No! That would be too severe! To execute them! Merciful Heaven, what a gruesome idea! Heinrich Döring, Friedrich Gleich, Wilhelm Blumenhagen, Methusalem Müller *—oh my teeth are chattering, my teeth are chattering! (*Heaving a sigh of relief*) Ah, here comes the Schoolmaster with the wine!

(*Enter the Schoolmaster and Little Gottlieb, each loaded down with wine bottles.*)

SCHOOLMASTER (*sings*): Vivat Bacchus, long live Bacchus, Bacchus was a wonderful man! (*To Little Gottlieb*) Sing, you silly dolt, sing along!

LITTLE GOTTLIEB (*quacks*): Vivat Bacchus, long live Bacchus, Bacchus was a wonderful man!

MUSHCLIFF: Little Gottlieb, you croak so badly the stones wish they had ears they could stop up.

SCHOOLMASTER: Heh, heh? Hasn't the boy a most delectable voice? I have twenty-two letters from the Sirens lying on my desk. They absolutely must have him for an engagement with their chorus. But each time I answer that he's still too young.

---

* Döring, Gleich, Blumenhagen, and Müller were minor writers, biographers, translators, and publishers of the period. Müller edited the *Zeitung für die elegante Welt*, a journal ridiculed earlier in the play.

ACT THREE, SCENE 1

RATBANE: You long-nosed slave-driver, stop blustering and set out the glasses.

SCHOOLMASTER (*setting glasses on the table*): Here they are!

RATBANE: Hurry, and fill them up!

SCHOOLMASTER: Patience! Patience! Just half a minute! (*He runs to the bed, pulls off a bed-sheet, and wraps it around his head.*)

MUSHCLIFF: Zounds, Mr. Schoolmaster, what kind of a mad disguise is that?

SCHOOLMASTER: Mere precaution, Mr. Mushcliff, mere precaution! I like to do my drinking with a bandaged head, in case I fall down.

MUSHCLIFF: Oh wise, seasoned veteran! As your humble disciple, I will copy your precautionary measures forthwith!

RATBANE: And me, too! I'll do the same! (*They tear loose two sheets and wrap them the same way around their heads.*)

SCHOOLMASTER: Indeed, Gentlemen, in these monstrous bed-sheets our three heads look like three unfortunate flies in the middle of a milk bucket.

MUSHCLIFF: Schoolmaster, tell us a story from your youth.

RATBANE: Yes, yes, from your youth. (*They sit around the table and fill their glasses.*)

SCHOOLMASTER (*drinks*): "*Fuimus troes*" *—"We were Trojans"!—the golden years of youth are gone!—Little Gottlieb, where are you?—Open your snout, you lout! A gulp of Germanized champagne won't do your patriotism any harm! Now, Gentlemen, to proceed with this tale out of those *tempi passati* is a ticklish undertaking for a schoolmaster who must maintain the respect of his pupils, and for a married man whose wife is plagued by jealousy!

MUSHCLIFF: No prefaces! You've been in love! You must tell us about your first love!

RATBANE: Huh!—How it thrills our dried-out pedagogical billy goat to hear you mention his first love!

---

* Virgil's *Aeneid*, Canto II, v. 325.

SCHOOLMASTER: O you beautiful, passionate-romantic, never-to-return-again days of the vanished past when I—Here's mud in your eye, Gentlemen. Long live little Hannah Honeysweet!

MUSHCLIFF and RATBANE: Here's mud in her eye!

SCHOOLMASTER: Forgive me, but I treasure this girl so immeasurably that I find it impossible to be content with drinking only a single glass to her health! *(He drains six glasses in a row.)*

RATBANE and MUSHCLIFF: Bravo, Schoolmaster! We too know how to appreciate your little Hannah! *(They likewise drain six glasses.)*

SCHOOLMASTER: And now that we've all properly honored little Hannah, I shall get on with my story. The sweet child was an angel, but her father, the headmaster of the local city school, was nothing but a shabby filou. He wore a wig which, tied at the back, dogs and cats used to chase from early dawn until midnight, mistaking it for a rat's nest. While his worn-out leather breeches were once cited by one of our historians, in a learned dispute over the oldest traces of German commerce with foreign peoples, as a Phoenician mausoleum.

RATBANE and MUSHCLIFF: Hoho! A mausoleum! *(They drink.)*

SCHOOLMASTER *(to Little Gottlieb, who stands idle in a corner)*: You malicious, envious, cold-blooded, treacherous young monkey, why are you standing there in the corner? Why don't you open your mouth? You certainly don't expect to stay sober and mock our carousing, do you? Drain this bottle, *stante pede,* or I'll bite off your left thumb! *(Little Gottlieb grabs the bottle and downs it with great glee. The Schoolmaster turns back to Ratbane and Mushcliff.)* Well, so this headmaster was a harpagon *—an old skinflint—and we students hated him as much as we loved his daughter. But since I was a bright lad, and he needed company to help him while

---

* The correct Latin form is *harpago,* i.e., boathook or grappling iron, used metaphorically by Plautus and Molière for "miser" or "skinflint."

away the time on long winter evenings when he never burned a candle, I was quite in his favor, and had to visit him regularly as night fell. There in the dark room I would sit with him and his daughter—he on my left, she on my right. While prattling about his editions of Pliny, I would manage furtively to press her soft, baby hand. After feeling her response, I would go further, gradually wind my arm about her dainty neck, tug at her neckerchief, and finally finger her without inhibition between the legs. One night, to my great distress, the old man sat in her place. I, unaware of the change, began as usual to finger "her." To be sure, little Hannah's strange, tough leathery dress did strike me as odd, but I, in my infatuated blindness, would not let myself be deterred. The headmaster himself, whose wife had been dead for some time, probably enjoyed my tendernesses, for he didn't lift a finger and remained still as a mouse. But finally, when I whispered in his ear "Hannah child, Hannah child, how come so ugly tonight!" this affront to his beauty threw him into such a rage he dealt me a blow on the face that not only yanked me out of my deceptive illusion, but his fist left such a powerful imprint upon my cheek that the next day everybody wanted to know if those marks had been tattooed on.

MUSHCLIFF *(half-tipsy)*: Delightful, Schoolmaster, delightful! So you fingered the old headmaster's *Lederhosen*! O joy! O joy! O joy!

SCHOOLMASTER: Long live fingering!

MUSHCLIFF: Let it live on! *(They souse without restraint.)*

SCHOOLMASTER: Jiminy Cricket, Mushcliff, look at Ratbane's heavy, bleary eyes!

RATBANE *(in his drunkenness, gripping the Schoolmaster by the vest)*: Aren't they? Isn't that right? Aren't my poems the dullest, tritest, most scrawling mess you ever saw—worthy only to be spat upon?

SCHOOLMASTER: They're every bit as good as the poetry of Elise von Hohenhausen, née von Ox.*

RATBANE: Crush me, pulverize me, Schoolmaster, trample me underfoot. I'm a worm, an unworthy nincompoop! My verse contains no sap, my thought no sense! I'm a worm, a worm, a tiny, little worm! Fling me into the swamp! Into the swamp!

SCHOOLMASTER *(who has been drinking continuously and gradually getting as plastered as the others)*: Do not weep, little Ratbane. Speak softly so that the nightwatchman doesn't hear! You're ranting! Your heart's overflowing!—Is't not so, Mushcliff?

MUSHCLIFF *(embracing the Schoolmaster)*: Ah Liddy, my Liddy!

SCHOOLMASTER *(girlishly)*: Don't crumple my bodice, Karl dear! *(Pointing to Little Gottlieb, who has emptied his bottle and now comes reeling out of the corner)* But hide yourself, dearest friend, hide! Here comes my father!

MUSHCLIFF: I fear you're a trifle drunk, Liddy!

SCHOOLMASTER: Unfortunately, dearest Karl, I've peered a little too deeply into the glass!

RATBANE *(falling to the floor)*: "Folly, thou triumphst, and I cease to be!" † *(He falls asleep.)*

LITTLE GOTTLIEB *(scrambling up the Schoolmaster and looking into his face)*: You naughty Schoolmaster, you! You thrashed me! You hit me! Scolded me! I'm drunk! I'll hit you back! I'll hit you back!

SCHOOLMASTER: O most honored Father! Forgive me! O forgive

---

* Elisabeth Philippine Amalie, Freifrau von Hohenhausen, geborne von Ochs (1789–1857), author of poems, tales, and novels, translations of Byron and Scott. During 1822–1824 she was a member of Berlin literary circles, where she instituted her famous evening literary teas. Later she criticized Grabbe's works in the Mindener *Sonntagsblatt*.

† Spoken by the dying Talbot in Schiller's *Jungfrau von Orleans*, Act III, Scene 6.

ACT THREE, SCENE 1

me! I cannot help it. I must marry my Karl or I shall die! Be not so cruel, most magnanimous of fathers! On bended knee, I beseech you, be not so cruel to your unhappy daughter! *Pardonnez-moi, Monsieur!*

MUSHCLIFF: Yes, My Lord, pardon us, and hinder not our temporal and eternal bliss!

(*Little Gottlieb tumbles head-over-heels onto the floor.*)

SCHOOLMASTER (*happily*): Victory, victory! He pardons us. He tumbles to the floor! Karl, Karl, come to my arms! We may love each other!

MUSHCLIFF (*inspecting Little Gottlieb*): Now that I look a little closer at your honored father, he seems to have become a hell of a lot smaller than of old!

SCHOOLMASTER: He's had the measles, my beloved!

MUSHCLIFF: Ugh! Ugh!

SCHOOLMASTER: Good God, why do you sigh?

MUSHCLIFF: Woe, woe is me! I'm afraid I'm going to fall under the table!

SCHOOLMASTER: Then, frankly, I can give you no other advice than to climb onto it. (*Mushcliff climbs onto the table so as not to fall off, and then falls down under it. The Schoolmaster raises a horrible cry and claps his hands together over his head.*) O fate, fate, unrelenting fate! No human cunning can ward you off, no mortal can escape you! Mushcliff climbs *up* on the table, and yet, all that notwithstanding, he has to fall *down*! O fierce, stone-hearted monster! (*He grinds his teeth.*)

MUSHCLIFF: Will no one help me up? Schoolmaster! Liddy! Where are the two of you?

SCHOOLMASTER: *Zaïre, vous pleurez?* * That pains me, upon my honor, that pains me!—*Venez, ma chère!* It's pitch-black outside! Let's go to church and play the organ! (*He takes Mushcliff by the arm and waddles off with him.*)

---

* Voltaire's *Zaïre*, Act IV, Scene 2.

SCENE 2

A meadow, daybreak.

Baron Murdrax is out taking a walk, meets thirteen apprentice tailors, puts on his napkin, and kills the whole lot.

SCENE 3

A Room in the Village

(Enter the four Natural Scientists, their heads bleeding, each with a flintstone in his hand.)

ALL FOUR TOGETHER: There, we've deliberately cracked our heads and racked our brains with these flintstones and still cannot determine what kind of fellow that finger-in-the-flame-sticking so-called Bishop is! Oh! Oh! Oh!

ONE OF THEM: Do not despair, Gentlemen! Science calls! Let us try once more! Courage! Let's crack our heads and rack our brains again!

ALL FOUR: Once again: crack our heads, rack our brains! *(They strike their heads with the flintstones—with a vengeance—get nothing out—and exit, cursing.)*

(Enter the Schoolmaster with Mushcliff and Ratbane.)

SCHOOLMASTER: What a crazy night! When I woke up, I found to my astonishment that I was lying in the church at the foot of the organ, right in front of the pedals.

MUSHCLIFF: And I was sitting, legs akimbo, on the sarcophagus of the baronial family vault.

RATBANE: I was lying under your desk, Schoolmaster, and little Gottlieb was next to me, snoring like a badger.

SCHOOLMASTER: It is now my humble suggestion that each of us partake of a light morning snack. It will dissipate the aftermath of inebriation or, to put it more elegantly, drive away our hangovers.

RATBANE: I am most distressed that I cannot join you. I have a commission to perform for the Baroness that brooks no delay. *(Exits.)*

SCHOOLMASTER: Ratbane is a fool. If he knew the voluptuous joy—after drinking all night—of eating a nicely salted herring, bones and all, and then washing it down with straight rum at the corner tavern, he wouldn't give a damn about his commission!

MUSHCLIFF: I shall go with you, Schoolmaster! Come! I have an enormous appetite! *(Both exit.)*

SCENE 4

A Room in the Castle

(Enter Ratbane and Liddy.)

RATBANE: No, Miss Liddy, do not deny my request—consent to a drive in the woods. Lopsbrunn is one of the most fascinating places on earth. Like a shepherd's hut out of Guarini's *Pastor Fido*,* it lies in the green solitude of the oak forest.

---

* Referring to *Il pastor fido*, a pastoral play by Giovanni Battista Guarini (1538–1612).

Like two liquescent nightingales, two murmuring brooks twitter through the stilly purlieu of their surroundings, and, as an assiduously poeticizing Count * so feelingly expressed it, pilgrims bloom there behind the bushes and murmur sweet sylvan prayers in the forest shrine!

LIDDY: Nicely declaimed, Mr. Ratbane!—How far is it to Lopsbrunn?

RATBANE: Not quite a mile, and the way alternates charmingly between leafy hillocks and grassy vales.

LIDDY: Be prepared then. The carriage should be made ready within the hour, and we can drive to the hunting lodge with my uncle. *(Exits with Ratbane.)*

SCENE 5

Thick Woods—Evening

(Enter the Schoolmaster with a giant bird cage on his back.)

SCHOOLMASTER: The sun has gone down, and the tired world has put on its starry nightcap. Half the earth now seems dead; behind curtains, nightmares terrify unprotected sleep. Magic begins its dread work in the service of the pale Hecate. Murder, roused by her howling nightwatcher, the wolf, slinks about her hideous business in giant robber-strides. The Blacksmith has put together a cage for me which I shall set up here in this bushy thicket. The axe-blows of the wood-stealing Devil

---

* Meaning Otto Heinrich Graf von Loeben, called Isidorus Orientalis (1786–1825), a pseudoromantic poet and novelist. This is probably a take-off on his pastoral-chivalric novel, *Arkadion* (1811–1812), or on his poems of a "contemplative pilgrim."

ACT THREE, SCENE 5

echo in the distance, and I shall have greatly deceived myself if the magical effect of sixteen condoms does not lure him here! * (*He sets the cage in the shrubbery, opens the door, places the condoms inside, and then steps off to the side. A pause, and then the Devil enters, sniffing.*)

SCHOOLMASTER: Ha, here he is already! How they tickle his nose!

DEVIL: I smell two quite different things here: on my left, something lascivious, child-contracepting—on my right, something drunken, child-solicitous.

SCHOOLMASTER: I'll be damned! He can't mean *me*, can he?

DEVIL (*while moving toward the condoms*): The lascivious lures me powerfully on—(*Turning toward the Schoolmaster*) but the drunken baits me no less—(*Standing still*) if only I knew which of the two were more immoral! (*He sniffs harder.*)

SCHOOLMASTER (*in great anxiety*): By the Devil, my conscience!

DEVIL: I have it! The drunken, child-solicitous thing to my right is far worse. The licentious, child-contracepting thing to my left is, by comparison, innocence itself! (*He rushes over to the Schoolmaster.*)

SCHOOLMASTER (*as he backs away from him in a circle*): Holy Sacrament, now I'm in a fine mess! I never dreamt I could be more sinful than a condom! † It's nothing but simple calumniation by the malicious Mr. Mephistopheles!—Thank God, here's a piece of church pew I must have stuck into my coat pocket in my drunkenness last night! I'll brandish it in his face and frighten him away! (*He does so.*)

DEVIL (*sneezes violently and recoils*): Phew! The drunken thing

---

* In previous editions, this passage reads: "and I shall greatly have deceived myself if the magical effect of three volumes of Jacob Casanova de Seingalt, published by Wilhelm von Schutz, does not lure him here! Just to make sure, however, I shall intensify the effect with the posthumous writings of the late Althing and spread them on the Casanova like bad pepper on fat ham." (Althing wrote obscene tales and translated Lesage's *Gil Blas*.)

† Here, other editions read: "I never dreamt I could be more sinful than the *Memoirs* of Jacob Casanova de Seingalt and Althing's *Posthumous Writings!*"

has bettered itself with a piece of church pew! Phew!— Nay, now I'd rather turn back to the licentious thing, even though it be more moral! *(He runs eagerly back into the cage, and, just as he picks up the condoms in his hand, the Schoolmaster jumps up and slams the door behind him.)*

DEVIL *(crying out)*: O ye elements, they've locked me in—I'm caught! *(Violently rattling the bars)* In vain! In vain! The bars are laid in the shape of a cross, I cannot break them! *(Looking at the Schoolmaster)* Oh, you rascally, swindling, mean—No, I meant to say: you sweet, lovable, most worthy man! Let me out! Oh, set me free!

SCHOOLMASTER: Go whistle for it! With bacon, you catch mice —with condoms, the Devil! *(He picks up the cage, sets it on his back, and carries off the Devil.)*

(Enter Baron Murdrax with his accomplices.)

MURDRAX *(clears his throat and spits before beginning his speech)*: Comrade accomplices! Baroness Liddy is lounging over there in the hunting lodge at Lopsbrunn! Inasmuch as she does not want to accept my amicable wooing, I am determined to abduct her, with your help, *par force!*—Have you brushed your hair over those gallows-physiognomies of yours so that I need not feel ashamed of you?

THE ACCOMPLICES: We have.

MURDRAX: Good.

(They exit. Enter Mushcliff with three armed servants.)

MUSHCLIFF: Suspicious hordes sneak through the forest—Miss Liddy and her Uncle are at Lopsbrunn. I fear, I fear in the wind a conspiracy against her! *(To the servants)* Load your pistols. Perhaps you'll have a chance to burn your mark on some scoundrel's skin! *(They load their pistols and go off.)*

SCENE 6

A Bare Room in the Hunting Lodge at Lopsbrunn

(Enter Liddy, the Baron, and Ratbane.)

LIDDY: Ratbane, you have misled us horribly!—If it's romantic here, then—ugh! Ooh, Uncle dear, I'm frightened! Order the carriage, and let's get out of this bandits' lair!
BARON: Why, child, you're trembling! That isn't at all like you!
LIDDY: I beseech you, harness the horses! Harness the horses!
BARON: Hello there! Mine host! *(Enter the Host.)* Have you fed my horses?
HOST: I don't feed strange horses! *(Exits.)*
LIDDY: Old grumpy!
BARON *(rushing after him)*: You miserable churl, now you *will* feed them!
LIDDY: Uncle, Uncle, where are you going? He doesn't hear me and goes storming down the steps!—And not even a light in this gloomy room! . . . Ratbane, where are you?
RATBANE *(with pinched voice)*: I—dear lady, I—
LIDDY *(startled)*: Heavens, what was that? What a clatter!
RATBANE *(teeth chattering)*: Probably only a mouse that ran across the floor.
LIDDY: Oh, I almost fear my own breath!—I've never felt such dread before. At last! Here comes Uncle with a light!
BARON *(rushing in violently, a lamp in his hand)*: Ratbane, show me your face! *(After lighting it up)* No, you know nothing about it! I absolve you!
LIDDY: By all the saints, what does this mean?
BARON: That host is a treacherous rogue, Niece! He allows a mob dressed up like robbers into the house and refuses me my horses!

LIDDY: Jesus! We are lost! *(She sinks into a chair.)*
RATBANE *(in despair)*: Lost! Lost!
BARON: And if those robbers were only after our money—but they're determined to have you, Liddy, you!
RATBANE: Oh, if that's all it is, Liddy, then save us! Save our lives! Necessity knows no law! If you grant the bandit captain a private audience, the possible ensuing complications can be easily disposed of by a so-called trip to a spa.
LIDDY: Shut up, you miserable versifier, shut up, and hide your worthless self over there behind that stove! *(Pulling out a hatpin)* Let a single one of those villains dare so much as touch my hand, then this hatpin shall penetrate my breast ten times! . . . On your feet, dear Uncle! Barricade the door! In danger, the weakest is often the strongest!
BARON: Noble, heroic child! *(They barricade the door.)*
LIDDY: Shove the table in front of it!
BARON: It's too heavy for us.
LIDDY: Then I'll carry it myself!
BARON: Liddy, Liddy, that enormous table will crush you!— In the name of the Lord, where do you get all that strength?
LIDDY: Take this dagger and give me your hunting knife!—Ha, they're coming!

(Baron Murdrax and his accomplices storm the door and, after several kicks, break it down. Liddy throws the hunting knife at the head of one of them; the mob stops short for a moment. Shortly afterward Mushcliff's voice is heard, pistol shots ring out, the attackers scatter and flee. Mushcliff bursts in, and his servants follow with the captured Baron Murdrax.)

LIDDY: We're saved! *(She faints in Mushcliff's arms.)*
MUSHCLIFF *(to the Baron, pointing to Murdrax)*: There's the ringleader of this dastardly raid—*(Enter two servants with Sir Wattsdale.)*—and, as Baron Murdrax admits, that one, whom we found lurking nearby, sold the Baroness for about twenty thousand Reichstaler to an innkeeper-and-bride collector. Also,

ACT THREE, SCENE 6

he very carefully stuffed all his pockets full of onions so that later he'd be able to ring tears of commiseration from his eyes.

(*The servants turn out Wattsdale's pockets, and a mass of onions tumble forth.*)

LIDDY (*recovering*): You, Mushcliff, you risked your life for me. If my hand can serve as recompense, it is yours.
MUSHCLIFF: Blissfully happy, I sink at your feet—
LIDDY: Not so! A man like you need humble himself before no woman! Joyfully I press this marriage kiss upon those lips you yourself so unjustly used to mock!
BARON: Well done! I bless your union!
RATBANE: And I shall prepare the epithalamium!
LIDDY (*smiling*): Ratbane, you are a shocking coward!
RATBANE: I am a poet, dear lady!
BARON (*to Wattsdale and Murdrax*): But you, you wretches, you are a disgrace to the nobility, you shall suffer inexorably the punishment you so well deserve! I'm going to have you two bound together like the lowest of criminals, I'll have you driven into town at high noon, I'll have you—
MURDRAX (*getting heated*): Death and damnation! This overtaxes my patience! You want me bound and dragged into town! Ho ho, is that the thanks I get for so divinely playing my part? Do you think, Mr. Theater Baron, I didn't know you were the Actor V, and that you aren't permitted to lift a finger against me?—Quick, Wattsdale, let's climb down into the orchestra pit with the musicians—they are intimate friends of mine and wouldn't harm a hair on our heads.

(*Murdrax and Wattsdale clamber down into the orchestra pit. Enter the Schoolmaster; the cage holding the Devil, is on his back.*)

SCHOOLMASTER: Congratulations, Baron, upon your and your niece's lucky escape from the clutches of Baron Murdrax.

BARON: Am I in my right mind, Schoolmaster? Isn't that the Bishop you're dragging along in that cage?

SCHOOLMASTER *(sets the cage on the table)*: Hm, if the Devil be a man of God, then he might as well be a bishop, for this frosty chimney sweep is none other than Satan in person!

ALL PRESENT *(including Baron Murdrax and Wattsdale in the orchestra pit, call out in astonishment)*: What? Satan? Wonder of wonders!

SCHOOLMASTER: Yes, for the second time I've redeemed the oppressed Earth from this creature, and now I deliver him, like a sparrow in a cage, to mankind, to be disposed of at its pleasure.

DEVIL: Baron, I implore you: let me out of this cage, free me from the Schoolmaster! He teases me endlessly, runs me through thick and thin, tickles me with long, stinging nettles, and sprinkles sand on my head three times every minute—

SCHOOLMASTER: It's the Devil, Baron. He deserves it. He deserves it. Everyone give me your attention! I shall now test him with my supreme experiment! First, I shall make him eat this hymnal, and then give me his paw. *(He holds the hymnal out to the Devil)* Eat! *(The Devil bristles up, resists.)* Eat it, Hound of Heaven, eat it! *(The Devil resists all the more violently.)*

(Enter a servant.)

SERVANT: A beautiful young lady who, judging from her dress is Russian, has appeared in the hallway, no one knows how.

DEVIL *(shouting with joy)*: Oh, that's my grandmother! That's surely my grandmother! And she's wearing a Russian fur outfit because she's afraid of catching cold!

RATBANE: That's where you're wrong, Mr. Satan! The servant's not talking about your grandmother, but about a lady who's still young and beautiful!

DEVIL: You fool! As if my grandmother were old and ugly! Don't you know that we immortals stay eternally young? If in spite of this I have nevertheless become old and shriveled, that is due to the special grief I suffered over the invention of Rumford soup kitchens for the poor.*

(Enter the Devil's grandmother, a ripe woman, dressed in a stylish Russian winter suit. She greets the party with a silent bow.)

DEVIL'S GRANDMOTHER: Schoolmaster, let my grandson out of that cage, and you may demand what you will in return for this favor.

SCHOOLMASTER: Then I demand that he give me his paw, Your Serene Highness.

DEVIL'S GRANDMOTHER: Give him your paw! *(The Devil gives his "paw" to the Schoolmaster, whereupon the latter lets him out of the cage.)* Come, my dear grandson, cheer up! They've wound up spring-cleaning down in Hell! So you can come right back home with me. There's steaming hot coffee all ready on the table, waiting to warm you up.

DEVIL: Splendid, little Grandmother, splendid!—But I do like to have something to read with my coffee!—Schoolmaster, do you have on you by chance any of Dr. Krug's works,† preferably one touching upon the latest developments in the Greek affair?

SCHOOLMASTER: Why, yes, they sent me some rotten red herrings today. Thanks to these same rotten herrings—*(While he pulls out several packages)* I can offer you *Tales* by van der Velde, ‡ the *Collected Works* of Luise Brachmann, who

---

* Benjamin Thompson, Count Rumford (1753–1814), noted British-American scientist, philanthropist, and administrator, was responsible for the invention of a cheap, nourishing soup.
† Wilhelm Traugott Krug (1770–1842), until 1834 Professor of Philosophy in Leipzig. Grabbe heard some of his lectures and is here satirizing Krug's polemical writings on current events.
‡ Franz Karl van der Velde (1779–1824), popular writer of his day of tales and historical novels in the style of Sir Walter Scott.

drowned herself,* and, if I'm not mistaken, even Goethe's *West-Östlicher Divan* and *Wilhelm Meisters Wanderjahren*.

DEVIL: Oy, what a pile of printed rubbish!—Grandmother, didn't you bring along a servant who could carry all this for us?

DEVIL'S GRANDMOTHER: Certainly, I brought Emperor Nero. He's outside on the steps cleaning your riding boots, which I also brought along.

DEVIL (*calls*): Nero! Nero!

(*Enter Nero, the Roman Emperor, in livery, the Devil's riding boots in his hand.*)

NERO: Your Grace called?

DEVIL: Hand me those boots! (*He pulls them on. Then, to Nero*) What's your friend Tiberius doing these days?

NERO: He's lying out on the bleaching lawn drying his laundry.

DEVIL: The smart thing to do! . . . Here, my good Nero—put the Greek affair under your left arm, the poetic works of Luise Brachmann under your right, and lug them along after us.

NERO: Very good, Your Grace!

DEVIL (*to the rest of the company, with a roguish smile*): Au revoir! We shall meet again. (*He, his grandmother, and the Emperor Nero, with books under his arms, all vanish into the earth.*)

SCHOOLMASTER: What was that, Baron?

BARON: That's what I'm asking *you*, Schoolmaster!

RATBANE: Which gives me an idea for a naively mad ballad: "Nero Cleans the Devil's Riding Boots"!

BARON: Are you not amazed, Liddy?

MUSHCLIFF: Liddy and I haven't been paying too much attention.

---

* Luise Brachmann (1777–1822), poetess and story writer, was inspired and influenced by Novalis, and committed suicide by throwing herself into the Saale near Halle. She, too, was a member of the Dresden "Liederkreis."

BARON: That's to your credit, it becomes lovers! (*To a servant who enters*) Is our carriage undamaged?
SERVANT: No human hand has touched it.
BARON: Then go fetch the wine basket from the carriage. (*Exit the servant.*) Let's have a few bowls of punch to revive ourselves.
SCHOOLMASTER (*thunderstruck*): Baron, how wise you are!

(*The servant brings in the wine basket.*)

RATBANE (*at the window*): But who's that coming through the woods down there with a lantern? He seems to be wending his way here!
SCHOOLMASTER (*likewise at the window*): Oh, let lightning strike! Imagine that fellow coming here through the woods late at night, lantern in hand, to help us drink up the punch! Why, it's that accursed Grabbe, or, as he really ought to be called, that Pigmy crab, the author of this play! He's as stupid as an owl, insults every other writer even though he's good for nothing himself, has crooked legs, is cross-eyed, and has the insipid face of a monkey! Shut the door on him, Baron, shut the door in his face!
GRABBE (*outside the door*): Oh you damned Schoolmaster! You boundless liar!
SCHOOLMASTER: Shut the door on him, Baron, shut the door in his face!
LIDDY: Schoolmaster, Schoolmaster, how embittered you are against the man who created you! (*Sound of knocking.*) Come in!

(*Grabbe enters with a lighted lantern.*)

The curtain falls.

END

WARNER MEMORIAL LIBRARY
EASTERN COLLEGE
ST. DAVIDS, PA. 19087